UNHALING

UNHALING

ON GOD, GRACE, AND A PERFECTLY IMPERFECT LIFE

By Elise Seyfried

ISBN 978-0-578-05056-0

INTRODUCTION

Unhale: v. To breathe out. To let go. Opposite of inhale.

(coined by my four year old son)

My name is Elise Seyfried, and I'm the Director of Spiritual Formation at Christ's Lutheran Church. Now, everyone knows Christian educators are supposed to be confident, competent, faith-filled and serene. And that may be true of 99% of them.

This is the story of the other one.

I am:

Perpetually sweaty-palmed, driven by equal parts coffee, panic and guilt

Hugely risk-averse (while taking the biggest risk of all—parenting five kids)

Owner of workout clothes I'll never wear, a piano I'll never be able to play, and a house that, for some reason, will never clean itself

Living a cluttered, overgrown, wildly disorganized, perfectly imperfect life.

These essays are snapshots of that life, and musings on the wonder of God's grace through it all. They were originally published in Christ Lutheran's monthly newsletter in the form of letters to the congregation. The essays are not ordered chronologically. Sometimes, therefore, my children seem to be getting younger as the book progresses. I do, too. I wish.

My profound thanks and love to my husband, children, and sister, to my dear friends and church family, and ultimately to God, for making this book (and this life) possible, and for reminding me, every once in awhile, to "unhale."

TABLE OF CONTENTS

MNEMONIA

"Do not trust your memory; it is a net full of holes; the most beautiful prizes slip through it."

--Robertson Davies

Just ran into a neighbor in the Acme supermarket. She was warm, friendly, and obviously knew who I was. I know this because she called me by name. As I stood there, squirming by the freezer case, 10 different names for this woman crossed my mind. Jennie? Jeanie? Joanie? Bob? (Well, maybe not Bob). I ended the conversation, which was filled with references to a husband and kids whose names I also could not recall, by calling her "honey." This was a cop-out, though not out of character for me. I am a "sweetie-honey" sayer by nature. In this regard, I would do well as a waitress at the Melrose Diner ("More coffee, hon?") Anyhow, I walked away from the encounter distressed.

On to the cereal aisle, where I stood for several minutes trying to summon up daughter Julie's special request. Mini-wheats? Frosted flakes? All-bran? (Well, maybe not All-bran). Oh, I made a grocery list. I just didn't remember to bring it. At the checkout counter, I rifled through my purse frantically looking for A) my Acme Supercard, B) my American Express card and C) my car keys. All were located, but my concern was understandable, as I have left these three items on counters all over Southeastern Pennsylvania at one time or another.

To cap off this Adventure in Amnesia, I pushed the shopping cart up and down the lot looking for my car. How hard could it be to find an Elantra? Pretty darned hard when, as it turned out, I'd driven the minivan to the store.

I realize this malady is not uncommon with my fellow members of Club Menopause. Many of us enter rooms for unknown reasons, pour milk for absent children, wash our hair twice in the shower (just to be on the safe side). But for me, the sad thing is, I used to have a really good memory. Really. I could recall entire conversations from years past, what I wore on my first date with my husband Steve, my telephone number from 1961. And now, pfft. Gone with the wind.

It took me quite awhile to avail myself of various mnemonic devices—the little tricks that prop up a failing brain. And most of these, I still forget to use. One idea I did embrace: I kept journals for each of the kids when they were tiny, so I'd have a record of their cute sayings and doings. For years, they stayed securely in a bookcase in our room. As I write this, I have just found the journals, after a panicky 24+ hours of combing the house for them. They had migrated, quite logically, to the attic, under the Christmas ornaments. Of course, where else?

What we remember, and what fades away, fascinates me. It has nothing to do with desire, I've concluded. How else to explain that, 27 years after her death, I can no longer recall the sound of my sister Maureen's voice—yet the lyrics and tune of a 27 year old McDonald's jingle remain ever-fresh? How can I quote the children's plays Steve writes, chapter and verse, yet ALWAYS leave the oven on during dinner? It's quite annoying.

Where was I going with this? Just a second.

Oh, yes.

When I was little, I had what I firmly believed was a very strong memory of being in Heaven before my birth. There were the requisite clouds and angels, and a really benevolent, grandpa-ish God. Apparently I got to request my parents, and was sent down to earth on something resembling a playground slide. And, for awhile, this "memory" was as real to me as anything I knew. I knew that God had loved me before I was born. At some point I let go of this vision of Paradise, teeming with babies placing orders for their future families.

But I never let go of the feeling. The feeling of being loved before I could love anyone myself. Loved by my parents, certainly. But also loved by Someone else, before, during, and after my life.

So, I hold to the feeling, and the sense that I am me and no one else for a reason, whatever that reason might be. And as I stumble and slip absent-mindedly through this world, I sometimes wander into a profound Truth: that I may be adding something memorable to the human story just by living my life. God is using me daily (and if ever there was a leaky vessel for His grace, brother, this is it). Nevertheless, He finds a way to continue the story through me.

One of my favorite hymns is a relatively new one. Our church music director Ken plays it every Maundy Thursday. The title of it is "God Remembers." The lyrics remind us that God remembers pain. God remembers love. God remembers us.

And if God remembers, maybe I can relax when I forget.

SKYDIVING

"Surely God is my salvation; I will trust, and will not
be afraid..."

--Isaiah 12:2

"Look! Here they come!" The crowd gathers. A finger points upward;
we crane our necks to follow. Suddenly, appearing in the clouds, a
bright orange flash. Then a yellow. A green. A red. As we watch, the
shapes form—parachutes. Spread out like multicolor stars in a blue,
blue sky, they drift slowly down. From this distance, it is impossible to
see human forms attached to these beautiful bits of cloth. Seconds pass.
A minute. Now one chute, the first one seen, comes into sharper focus:
there are two people attached to one another, suspended in the air. A
tandem dive. Here comes a solo. Gradually the eight divers approach
the earth, arcing gracefully in the breeze. And now, at last, it is possible
to recognize individuals. There is my son Sheridan. There is my
daughter Rose. The ride is almost over. They come to rest in the grass,
surrounded by the billowy folds of their vivid parachutes. For the first
time in 20 minutes (or so it feels), I take a breath.

They walk towards the airport, grinning widely. They greet me,
words tumbling out fast—"awesome—so exciting—14,000 feet up—
the view was so gorgeous—freefall was the best—so cold up there—

felt unreal—can't wait to do it again!" I am only half-listening, because I'm still muttering "Hail Marys" under my breath. They are laughing, joking around, relaxed and happy. My sweaty fists have yet to unclench. They are safe. I am a wreck.

So what else is new?

Adventure and I have a long history of pursuit and escape—it chases me, and I do my best to stay far, far away. Life presents frequent opportunities to cast fear to the winds and go for it—"it" being just about anything involving heights, water, speed, tight places, darkness, physical agility, and the list goes on. My motto: "Just say no." The few times I have succumbed to pressure and given daring activities a whirl, I've been sorry. My first and last time snorkeling I was so seasick that, for the rest of my vacation, total strangers would come up to me and ask if I was feeling better. My first and last jungle canopy tour, in Costa Rica, I was so terrified of being in a harness in the air that I missed the tropical birds, the iguanas, the howler monkeys—indeed, I never once looked down, or around me (the whole point of doing this, I think). My idea of risk and thrills is going 30 in a 25 mile zone. I find it both amusing and dismaying to realize that every single one of my kids is a million times braver than me. As is my husband. They all love long hikes to high, rocky outlooks, where they stand at the edge of the precipice and relish the sight of the world beneath them. I am afraid to even look at the pictures they take.

At my age I don't anticipate a big change in my personality. Though they promise to take me with them on their daring escapades, my loved ones don't seriously believe I would ever join them.

But there was a moment, a fleeting moment, that glorious late-summer Sunday when I got a glimpse of something more. For an instant, I saw Sheridan and Rosie falling from the sky, and for an instant I forgot to be afraid. My children took a giant and literal leap of faith, out of a plane and down, down, down into a world they love and do not fear. A world where life can be risky, but promises a rush of joy for those who dare to take a few chances. I watched my children, turned them over to the God who cherishes them, and I forgot to panic.

That rainbow of divers floating down from the heavens was so beautiful.

And if my heart filled with the wonder of that moment, I could only imagine how my kids felt. The rush of icy air. The chute opens, and freefall slows to drift. And there are lakes and fields and roads, dotting the distant landscape. The sun is so bright. It is so good to be alive.

I can only imagine a life filled with that feeling. They don't have to imagine. The world is spread out below, and they can't wait to dive in to it all. God grant me the grace to let them go. Joyfully.

PIANO LESSONS

"Get up from that piano. You hurtin' its feelings."

-- Jelly Roll Morton

Cover your ears. I'm about to perform "Lady be Good" on the piano, and believe me, this lady is not good. Cover your ears, unless you have a taste for the sound of exquisitely wrong notes, banged out *fortissimo*. Actually, head for the hills, if you have any affection for music whatsoever. It's Sunday afternoon, and I am NOT ready for my lesson. Oh, I ran through the scales on, what was it, Monday, before work and again Wednesday after dinner. I put Gershwin up on the stand and gave him a stab (I heard him scream from beyond the grave). My sight-reading skills are inching infinitesimally forward, but I would still put myself in the "age four and under" category of proficiency—and that is patently unfair to the more advanced four year olds. I shouldn't still be muttering, "Every Good Boy Does Fine" every time I look at a line of music, should I? Just why am I doing this again?

Because I have a dream. I have a dream that one day I will wake up, walk over to the Yamaha and suddenly possess the hands of a prodigy. Gershwin will purr with delight; Beethoven will roll over. In my dream, I am Horowitz, I am Lang Lang. In my dream, my fingers dance over the keyboard, and people in neighboring houses drop their dishcloths to revel in the mellifluous sounds drifting out my window. In my dream, I don't need no stinking practice.

And because I have a son. A son who is my monumentally patient teacher. A son who, improbably, believes I can actually coax a tune from the piano, using nothing more than my thick and clumsy digits and my meager brain power. A son I would do absolutely anything not to disappoint. So I keep on trying.

I've been thinking about this enterprise, Elise vs. 88 keys, a lot lately. What's the deal? At 50, a career as a concert artist is implausible at best. I have reduced my ambition from Mozart concerti to the kind of sheet music decorated with balloons and clowns, and even then I may be overreaching. Every week, I swear I'll spend the time I need to prepare, the time I need not to waste Sheridan's. This time, I'll be ready to dazzle him. "Such arpeggios, Mom! Sheer genius!" And it's Sunday afternoon again, and I am a failure again. And I hate myself for perpetuating this cycle of incompetence, for being so unrealistic. I am a distracted middle aged woman with enough fish to fry. This is obviously too much for my skillet.

And every day I wake up from the dream that I did life right. I was thoughtful, friendly, courteous and kind. I cared for my loved ones tenderly, and did great gobs of outreach to the underprivileged as well. I did not fail my God, who patiently believes in me. Then I wake up. And it's Sunday afternoon, and Gershwin awaits. And I've failed again.

I used to think the victories, however small, were what mattered to God. The scale, the un-butchered line from *Porgy and Bess*. But now, with my piano lessons, I am learning something else.

God is the one who will still sit by me when I massacre Mozart and torture Tchaikovsky. He already knows I'm not ready for the lesson. He saw me miss practice. He knows I want to Be Perfect Now, and He laughs. Lovingly. Like a parent. Like a son. He thinks it's a hoot that I want to stretch in this new direction, and He's not about to shoot me down. He's seen the hundreds of ways I have cut corners, missed the mark, never made it out of the starting gate in life. He is with me at the bottom of the mountain, just as He is with those hotshots on the pinnacle. And if I never get past the foothills, He is with me still. Faithful, still. For, you see, He made this crazy would-be pianist, and maybe, just maybe, He knew what He was doing.

I will play in Sheridan's recital next spring, I swear. It might be the "Pathetique" Sonata. It will more likely be "Happy Birthday." But I will share the piano bench with Someone who never has given up on me. And never will.

CLUTTERED

"Out of clutter find simplicity."

-- Albert Einstein

My daughter Rosie was home a few weeks ago, and came upstairs from her former basement bedroom (now my younger daughter Julie's) with a huge, filled trash bag. "What's in there?" I asked. "Oh, just some old stuff I don't need anymore," was her breezy reply. It took me all of 10 seconds to be conquered by my curiosity. "Mind if I have a look?" "Moooom. You're just gonna save everything, and undo all my sorting… oh, all right, go ahead!"

The first valuable thing I came across was her essay on surfing, written as a high school freshman for speech and debate class. Then came a paper from her year as a foreign exchange student in Thailand. A hair elastic. Pens that surely still had a little life left in them. What finds!! I couldn't believe she was planning to chuck these treasures!! Little by little, the giant trash bag deflated as I salvaged item after item.

At last I finished, and squirreled it all away. The papers went into a large plastic tub that slides under my bed, filled to overflowing with the kids' schoolwork that I have saved—not sorted, mind you, just saved. The perfectly good hair elastic went into the bathroom drawer with the 30 other hair elastics already in residence. The dried-up pens, into the mug in the kitchen where, along with the lime green crayon, dry erase marker and pencil stub, they will join the family of useless writing implements by the phone.

I am a saver, unless it's something really important. Those things—money, jewelry, medical records—I tend to absentmindedly pitch. If my impulses are not checked, I will someday be the old lady whose house is packed with so much junk that she's featured on Action News.

And anyone who has had the treat of visiting my office at church knows just what I mean.

The other night when I couldn't sleep, I imagined some disaster that would force our immediate evacuation. If I had one minute to decide what, besides my family, to salvage, what would I choose? The collection of programs from every single play I attended for the past 30 years would absolutely need to come. The 998-piece puzzles, the Beanie Babies, the four sets of decorative cheese spreaders—all keepers. The shelf full of empty DVD cases (I probably absentmindedly pitched the DVDs themselves)—never know when we'll need those! As it turns out, I'd better have a moving van permanently in the driveway, standing by to cart away my priceless possessions should a sudden need arise. Semper paratus!

The day will come when I have nothing to do (yeah, right). On that day, I will approach the attic, ready at last to face the immense array of boxes, envelopes, bins and folders that live up there. That will be the day I finally catalogue everything, and summon the courage to wing "Christmas Cards 1978," as well as most of the 150 crayon drawings of a lighthouse at sunset that I have held onto from Sheridan's Naptime Art Period.

As they say, that will be the day.

In my heart I know it's only stuff. Life can so easily become a suffocating piling-up of things. We didn't bring it all with us, and we sure can't take it with us when we go, at the end of our earthly story. And while we're here, what a burden it all can be.

Maybe it's time to wrest a little order from the chaos, and replace that moving van with a dumpster.

No Mom can serve two masters. Can I loosen my grip on my possessions so that I can grab God's hand instead?

EXERCISING MY OPTIONS

"I am pushing sixty. That is enough exercise for me."

--Mark Twain

Isn't running wonderful? Racing through the streets in every season, pulse pounding, legs aching, body sweating…hooray for running. What a super way to get into shape!

And the gym! The perfect spot when the weather is inclement and you still want your hour or two of heart-rate-elevating activity. Treadmill, stationary bike, CNN on the big screen TV…what's not to love?

And exercise videos! My collection ranges from the classics (Jane Fonda, circa 1988) to *Awesome Abs in 10 Days* to a hip-hop kickboxing routine. A veritable library for the home fitness buff!

And now, summer, with its plethora of choices! Swimming, hiking, tennis, softball, hang gliding, surfing…a million ways to move in the great outdoors!

Not that I do any of this, mind you.

I hate exercise to the same degree that I love coffee—wildly, immoderately. Physical fitness, like decaf, is for others, those poor souls who want to live long, healthy lives.

Seriously, though, I know in theory that exercise has much to recommend it. For one thing, cute workout clothes. I'm trying to think of a second thing. Give me a minute. No, I've never had that "endorphine high" that the true athlete raves about. For me, working out is like hitting yourself in the head with a hammer. It feels so good when it stops.

For many years I kept in fairly decent shape by acting. Once in awhile I would attempt a class (yoga, jazzercise), attend sporadically, do poorly, and drop out. Nowadays it is only my perpetual state of nervous energy that keeps me relatively slim. Otherwise, I am a real computer potato, tappity-tapping away all day, getting up at work only to walk next door to the office, and then only when I can't convey the message by shouting. There will come a day when my legs will buckle beneath me, I'm sure, from lack of use. Until that day comes, I will probably exercise nothing but my flying fingers.

Why (and I can't be the first to have noticed this) are the things that are good for you so much harder and less appealing than the things that are bad for you? Why do I not power-walk down to visit a neighbor, munching a healthful apple? Why do I climb into the car for this one-block odyssey, munching a Dunkin Donut if one is handy? All the fitness statistics in the world have not, so far, altered my behavior a whit. I'm stuck, mired in my bad habits. The excuses are many, and spring quickly to my lips. And even if I tried to change now, I reason, it would take me forever to get into shape, and forever I ain't got.

My body is a precious gift from God, and I see fit to leave it under the bed collecting dust.

The Christian life is full of "exercises" that can be just so much easier to skip. Helping the homeless man on the street. Building the Habitat house. Serving at the soup kitchen. Visiting the shut-ins. These are not the activities that will enlarge a bank account, or aid a climb to the top. They are the acts of love that should take up much of our days, but it is all too tempting to let the world's priorities dictate our own.

And so the years pass. Our "giving" muscles get flabby. Our spiritual NordicTracks rust. We settle. We settle, when we know we are called to do and be more, so much more. Just as I know that I should exercise, at least a little bit. And I don't.

Maybe it isn't too late to try again. I can certainly make a start. Hang up the car keys and step away from the Twinkie. And while I'm at it, work on some of those other bad habits of mine (and they are legion). There is time, after all. I can honor the gift of my health, and do what I can to maintain it. I can push back against society's priorities, a worthwhile exercise if ever there was one.

And I can decide: how, physically and spiritually, will I shape my tomorrows?

HAMSTER LOVE

"But ask the animals, and they will teach you; the birds of the air, and they will tell you; ask the plants of the earth, and they will teach you; and the fish of the sea will declare to you. Who among all these does not know that the hand of the Lord has done this?"

--Job 12:7-9

There was never a time in my adult life when I wanted a pet. Even as a child, my single foray into the animal kingdom involved a creature relatively low on the food chain. Julius Caesar was a Woolworth's turtle whose brief sojourn at our house was marked by many distressing fungal infections (his, not ours) requiring medications purchased at 10 times the price of Julius himself. Quite soon, we came to bury Caesar (not to praise him).

Dogs, cats, birds—they all were either frightening, too noisy, or too darned much work to contemplate having in our home. I was lucky enough to marry a man who shared my feelings on this subject, luckier still to have a number of children who passed through their early years with nary a pet request. Oh, once or twice we gave in to a hermit crab: no work, no noise, no anything, all the fun and excitement of feeding and watering an empty shell! Rose replicated my disastrous reptilian experience with her purchase of Speed, another turtle. Speed, faced with the prospect of life in our pet-phobic home, soon hurled himself from his little rock, breaking his neck.

It wasn't until our fifth child, Julie, that we came face-to-face with a true pet lover. We tried to ignore the signs—she never met an animal of any size or shape that scared her or intimidated her, she loved animal movies, animal-patterned clothes, animal crackers—in the vain hopes that she'd grow out of these notions. But here we are, 10 years down the pike, and her love for all creatures, great and small, continues to grow.

We are still nowhere near giving in on a dog (Julie, if you are reading this, Mommy means it!) but we have made a few concessions, always with the proviso that <u>she</u> will remember to feed, water, clean the cage, etc. of any creature that she acquires. I have to say I have been more than impressed by the way Jules mothers her current pair of pets. Noah, her goldfish (a "one week wonder" won many months ago at a school carnival) continues to thrive. Her beloved hamster, Puffles, seems quite content, judging by the merry squeaks of the annoying little wheel she runs on all night. I still have trouble with the concept that Puffles lives in a spiffy cage with toys and treats, yet if we saw something that looked just like Puffles running across the kitchen floor, we'd be setting a trap. But Puffles belongs to Julie, so instead we break out the best hamster kibble.

Ever so slowly, I am beginning to change my attitude. Or more accurately, Julie is changing my attitude. Because she loves animals so, and because I love her so, I am seeing animals a little bit differently. The dogs that were just barking, shedding annoyances to me are becoming individuals, with many different personalities. A few, I have to admit, are pretty lovable. Most are still annoying, but progress is being made.

Is this small transformation happening in my heart really so different from the transformation of a heart that knows it is loved by God? When we open ourselves up to the remarkable possibility that <u>we</u> are treasures, it becomes easier and easier to do what we can to return that great love. From there, it becomes possible to treasure each other more, just because we know there is something lovable in each one of us. From there, it becomes at least possible to imagine a future world that is filled with love--love given, love received, love passed along to every one of us. And, OK, I concede that includes the ones of us with fins, fur and feathers too.

BIRTHING

"Birth is violent, whether it be the birth of a child or the birth of an idea."

--Marianne Williamson

Anyone who has had a baby in the past, oh, 45 or 50 years is familiar with Lamaze. Lamaze, I'm here to tell you, is the great lie perpetrated by, I guess, Monsieur Lamaze himself, and fed to pregnant women—who, at that point in pregnancy, will eat pretty much anything. Briefly, it is a method of controlled breathing that purports to drastically diminish, if not completely extinguish, labor pain. How fabulous, and about time, right? The way to a pure, unmedicated, blissful birthing experience!

And so, during the 14th or 15th month of my first pregnancy, my loving partner (also known as "coach") and I, respectively, cheered and panted our way through "rehearsals" of the blessed event to come. We had an official Lamaze instructor, and fellow student/parents-to-be also cheering (the men) and panting (the beached whales) right along.

While the rest of me was heavy enough to move with a forklift, my heart was light as those telltale first twinges began. Right on schedule, the twinges escalated, and Coach Steve began the familiar litany, urging and encouraging. But wait! Something was horribly wrong! No one had remembered to tell the <u>baby</u> about Lamaze! There I was, huffing and puffing to beat the band, and yet in ever-increasing AGONY.

By hour nine, I was cursing M. Lamaze, my husband for his incredibly annoying pep talks, and myself for deciding to have children in the first place.

Lest you think I am one to learn a lesson from this (even as it became obvious my children all preferred to put me through the notoriously "uncomfortable" back labor), I panted and, later, screamed my way through Babies Two and Three. I bravely/stupidly rejected offers of medication because I had to prove myself to be heroic enough, strong enough, to take whatever my body could dish out. Number Three, Rosie, ever the drama queen, kept me waiting, and wailing, for my record of 14 hours before she arrived on the scene.

At 1:30 PM on May 15, 1991, Labor Number Four commenced. At 1:31 PM I got my epidural.

Now THAT was fabulous.

But honestly, aren't we all constantly giving birth? To ideas, to projects, to plans? And don't these births involve preparation, then delivery? And, let's face it, isn't a lot of it pretty painful? All too often, we latch on to our one way of doing things, our one way of looking at life (our Lamaze method, if you will), then close our eyes and grit our teeth and bear the consequences when our way just doesn't work. Help is out there, help is all around, but we're too lost in our intensity to even notice. And even if we do notice, we're too proud to accept assistance. To do that, we'd have to accept our inadequacy. Our weakness. Our limits. We'd have to actually humble ourselves, and who wants to do that?

Oh, wait. Jesus did. In a stable in Bethlehem. On the cross. And if God can humble Himself, why can't we? We are invited into the wonderful, topsy-turvy world of God's reality. Where the proud are brought low and the humble are not only helped, they are exalted.

So, the next time your labors are frustrating and ineffective, the next time your determination to be a be-all and end-all is challenged, rejoice. You have been given a chance to be helped. To reach out your hand and to be lifted up, and out of your troubles.

We never, after all, give birth alone. Our Coach is right beside us every time, offering us all the loving help we could ever need.

We just have to stop panting long enough to say "thank you."

ACTING THE PART

"The thing about performance, even if it's only an illusion, is that it is a celebration of the fact that we do contain within ourselves infinite possibilities."

--Daniel Day Lewis

A couple of years ago, I was strolling on the boardwalk at Rehoboth Beach with the family. I guess my, shall we say, audible voice could be heard above the din of the crowds and Funland rides, because a little one walking a ways behind us caroled, "Mommy! I hear Snow White!" I felt like quite the celeb, believe me. Angelina Jolie, eat your heart out.

Yes, I confess. In my "other life" I am Snow White. In fact, I am a parade of characters, ranging from Robin Hood's deputy to Peter Pan. As an actress in our children's theatre company, Family Stages, my "dress up" urges have been fully satisfied now for 25 years. While I am now not nearly as bouncy as I was in my prime, and my performances are quite rare these days, I can still troup on when the need arises. I realize that a 51 year old Cinderella requires more than the usual "willing suspension of disbelief," but I retain other skills that serve me well onstage. I may forget to pick up my child at soccer practice, but ask me any line from *The Wizard of Oz* and memory always serves!

Acting is an interesting job. It is a chance to inhabit another body, a different character than your own, make believe (and bring the audience along for the ride). It's a challenge to get there, but in the zone you can really lose yourself in the artificial reality of costumes and set. Scripted dialogue seems just like your own original utterances. Adrenaline enables surprising physical feats on the stage. I once fell and broke my wrist in the middle of a show, finished the whole show, THEN went to the hospital.

Of course, there is a danger in the profession of becoming too much of a chameleon, hiding your real self from the world by playing characters, indeed losing touch with who the "real you" might be. But isn't that a danger for us all at times? Isn't it easier to pretend to agree with an opinion we oppose? Don't we waste time just going through the motions of life, mouthing the same dialogue and repeating the same scenes day after day? Haven't we all woken up some mornings and asked ourselves who we really are?

If, to quote Shakespeare, "All the world's a stage, and all the men and women merely players," how does that make us feel? Maybe like bad actors, flubbing our lines and missing so many of our cues. Maybe trapped in a role we dislike, in a play we wish we could rewrite. Maybe powerless in the hands of some Great Producer-Director, who knows every step of our choreography before we dance.

But there is good news, fellow performers.

Perhaps the world can be seen as a stage on which the story of our lives is acted out. But we are free. Free to improvise as much as we like, to revel in the wonder of our being, and our being exactly where we are in time and space. The Lord has given us the reins, and lets us make our own choices every minute of every day. We don't have to be trapped by past behaviors. We don't have to continue to say, and do, and be, things we dislike. We can work on getting things right. And we can also relax and let ourselves flub our lines once in awhile. God never meant for us to savage our own performances like a nasty drama critic. He loves His ragtag band of players. He enjoys watching us live, and grow toward Him like flowers toward the sun, as we age, and learn.

Our play can be a glorious collaboration, with our fellow actors and with our God. We can weather the storms and sorrows of Act Two, believing that, when the curtain falls, a Heavenly ending awaits.

So go on, live your life with all the zest and joy it is in your power to create. Step into the spotlight with confidence, and make your story a beautiful one.

It's Showtime.

RAGE AGAINST THE MACHINE

"For a list of all the ways technology has failed to improve the quality of life, please press three."

--Alice Kahn

Working from home today, writing this on our shared home computer. The laptop is in for repairs, because—I'll try not to get too technical on you here—when you plug the thingy in, it (the laptop) doesn't think you did and the battery runs down. Or something like that. Toshiba will just have to figure it out. And having no laptop for two whole weeks is driving me insane!! It's almost as bad as getting halfway to the supermarket and realizing I left my cell phone at home! What will happen if I can't call the kids in Aisle 9 to see if we need bread? I don't think I want to find out.

We are not a super-techno family by many standards. Our TV is rather small and gimmick-free. Yes, we have no Blackberries. We have only just recently become part of the iPod universe. But I have discovered that, once a new electronic device enters our lives, it shows us who's boss pretty rapidly. And the boss ain't us. Was it really only eight years ago that I didn't know how to send an email? Now, when I am away from the Internet for even a day I fret and pace like an addict, fantasizing about the messages are piling up in my inbox—even the "fw:fw:fw: pass this one on!"s. The cell phone has also quickly become a necessity of life. God forbid if I don't have something in my purse that rings during a concert because I thought I'd put it on vibrate. I am a busy and important lady, and people need to <u>know</u> they can reach me 24/7!

My family and friends have heard me rail against the short attention spans and rudeness of many kids today—kids who walk through life with a constant soundtrack of music piped into earbuds, kids who see nothing wrong with texting each other in church. But I am being a hypocrite. I have clearly developed an equal (and equally annoying) reliance on machines—to feel connected, to feel better about, or at least more in control of, my world.

I have often heard people say that, if Jesus' ministry on earth was happening now, He would avail Himself of every possible modern device in order to get His message to us. And that may well be true. But it is all too easy for the medium to BE the message, and to lull us into thinking we really are connecting with one another. Do emails and pagers and cell phones make us closer? Or just make it easier for us to think we are? Are we hooked on instant communication—or instant gratification?

Growing a friendship, a deep, true friendship, takes time. It takes focus. It isn't a process well served by constant interruption, by easy distractions. In this world of the Next Big Thing, maybe we're losing a sense of the Real Big Thing: a grace-filled life, where there is room and time for a few deep, true friendships. Including friendship with the One who loves us the most.

I am so afraid we're losing that, with our ever-jangling cell phones and our red-hot computer keyboards. Though the wall-to-wall music in our ears can make this feel like a movie about life sometimes, this actually <u>is</u> life. Right now. And we can make our own choices, or let our machines shape our days for us.

Maybe it'd be a good idea for me to remember that. To go unplugged once in awhile, and just see what happens next.

OUR LATEST MOVE

"You are a hiding-place for me; you preserve me from trouble; you surround me with glad cries of deliverance."

--Psalm 32:7

You've lived in your house a looonnng time if…

1) you can remember having a slide shaped like an elephant in the back yard
2) also a wading pool
3) your child is almost 24
4) a tour of the house yields a wealth of memories, just based on the damage alone— scratches on the living room floor (tap dancing), the gouge in the wall behind the bunks (bed jumping), the crack in the garage window (lacrosse practice), the mysterious dent in the dining room table (still a mystery)
5) everyone has, at one time or another, slept in every bedroom
6) you haven't had to worry about new phone numbers or forwarded mail since 1988

Next June, we will have been in our house 20 years. Now, I realize in this area that is no record. Here, many people tend to remain in their neighborhoods, if not their same houses, for lifetimes. I remember being introduced to someone who told me she "wasn't from around here." She was, as it turned out, from neighboring Flourtown. Perhaps a foreign exchange program brought her to our Oreland. For me personally, our longevity is nothing short of remarkable.

I was not a child of the military; however, my dad was a salesman who quite often switched jobs. By the time I was a junior in high school I had attended eight schools in three states. Every couple of years it was time to pack up our duds and head on out to the next adventure. As we were pretty inept packers, even with all that practice, we left a trail of belongings wherever we went (or threw them away by accident in our moving frenzy).

Our dwellings tended to be a little on the quirky side. For quirky, read: bad heating systems, leaking roofs, bugs, and basements you could float a boat in every rainstorm. There was the poorly built apartment by the highway in Atlanta that shook with the passing of every vehicle outside. There was the isolated New England house beside the cranberry bog, 10 miles from town. Mom didn't drive; Dad was on the road all week. Perhaps we should have thought that one through. Then there was the New York house whose former owners had 14 children (yet only one bathroom)!

When Steve and I first married, the vagabond life continued for awhile. As actors, we lived where the work was: Alabama, Tennessee, Florida. Once we went on a children's theatre tour, and literally lived in motels for almost two years.

When we began our family, I wanted nothing more than to settle somewhere, to put down roots. We decided on the Philadelphia area and moved into a starter house in suburban Oreland. When Rosie came along and we outgrew our starter house, we moved one final time. And here we are to this day.

Staying in one place, especially to raise kids, has its definite advantages. One school system, one group of neighbors, one church. Yet there are times I long to break free, to call the moving company, to hit the open road once again. To get rid of half the stuff we own. To wake up in a new town, to meet all new people. Our children seem to have similar longings, now, though they will probably tell you they enjoyed not having to move, then. So far, the oldest three are in NYC, Annapolis, and Boston. They have seen France, Brazil, Thailand. Even Flourtown. And the world looks pretty good to them, pretty exciting. Settling down is for later—much later. Now is the time to look at Mom and Dad, waving, from the rear view mirror.

And so. Life. You move; you don't move. You know your surroundings intimately; you're constantly surprised by something new. So what is home? Home is not a zip code, new digs, or a residence of 20 years. Home is the feeling of belonging somewhere. Home is knowing someone is there for us, around the corner or around the globe. If we can think of God as a person, we can also think of Him as a place. Home. Our Home in the world, and beyond the world. A Home we can never leave, no matter where we go. Or where we stay.

Sometimes, I marvel at the depth of the roots I've put down, after all that wandering. And having been both, I still don't honestly know what I'd choose to be: oldtimer or newcomer. But as a child of God, I do know that wherever I am, there I am. Home.

THE ANTICHAPERONE

"For my thoughts are not your thoughts, nor are your ways my ways, says the Lord."

--Isaiah 55:8

You know what's tougher than reaching up, aspiring to roles for which you barely qualify?

Reaching down, trying to extricate yourself from roles you hate, when you are considered to be oh-<u>so</u>-qualified.

Case in point: I never (trust me) EVER aspired to the role of School Field Trip Chaperone. This is not to be confused with Church Mission Trip Chaperone. I love doing that, and who wouldn't? Those young people have a clearly defined sense of why they are going, and have hearts open to service. School field trip kids tend to operate with a different motto: Run, Hide, Scream, and Shop Till You Drop!

Oh, I figured I'd be a good soldier and take my occasional turn. One trip to Merrymead Farms with the kindergarten would be endurable, no? But surely Jarrettown Elementary could yield parents better suited, temperamentally and otherwise, to shepherd hordes of little angels through the museum and past the Great Historic Site.

It seems not. From preschool on, I have been the Go-To Mom when it came to steppin' out. Children's theatre, the mint, the science center—I've seen 'em all. Correction: They have all rushed past me in a fevered blur as my sweaty hands clasped two of my hyperactive charges while I endlessly counted the heads of the others. Hence, the Camden Aquarium will always be, for me, nothing more than the site of little Danny's clever escape attempt, hidden in the fauna of the rainforest exhibit. Baltimore's scenic Harborplace forever evokes a busload of 80 ebullient fifth graders, shrieking along to the "in-flight video"—Disney's *High School Musical*—on both ends of the trip. There are headaches no amount of ibuprofen can banish. That is one of them.

On these trips I have been, in many ways, the antichaperone—testy, agitated, petulant, bored. I'm the mom who won't let them shop, when clearly the rubber snakes at the zoo gift shop hold far, far more appeal than the real live reptiles. I am she who groans in impatience when she must search for yet another restroom, because her small group cannot, simply cannot coordinate their bladders. Yours truly: the spoilsport who refuses to join the other chaperone moms and kids for lunch at Hooters (call me a ridiculous prude, but 11 year old boys at Hooters is just creepy). No one seems that thrilled to have me along, adult or child, which has always suited me fine.

So why is it I am <u>always</u> chosen? And I do mean always. When there is a lottery of any other sort—you know, the sort involving money—my track record is below dismal. But I am quite the lucky girl when names are fished from the King Tut Exhibit bowl. I was even chosen to stroll through the art museum's Manet show with high school juniors, an experience only slightly less painful than the Baltimore Headache.

Perhaps there is a reason. Perhaps, God sees potential in me where I see none. It just may be that He thinks, if I stop kicking and screaming, I may discover something about myself. Cranky and querulous as I may be, I may be a good chaperone—good in the sense of keeping the kids safe and occupied, if not wild and free. For some of these tiny darlings, a small dose of tough love may be just what the doctor ordered. And maybe, I am here to provide it. God sees what I can't, what I don't want to see. And, time after time, puts opportunities in my path. It only remains for me to take the blinders off and embrace my fate.

Nah. Not ready for listening to God, not in this area. Not yet.

I think it's time to bring out the big guns. Next field trip I will wear a tutu, bare my teeth and snarl at the children, tell the teachers I wish I had a cushy job like theirs, flirt with the museum guards and steal little Danny's potato chips. Chaperone from Hell, that will be me.

It just might work. I may finally be outrageous enough to be stricken from the Big Book of Volunteers We Love.

And with my luck, the following week they will choose another chaperone for the touring production of *Hamlet*.

Starring Jude Law.

Darn. That God is clever.

TALK TO ME

"And this is the boldness we have in him, that if we ask anything according to his will, he hears us. And if we know that he hears us in whatever we ask, we know that we have obtained the requests made of him."

--1 John 5:14-15

"This comes to Evan Seyfried's voice mail."

How I dread hearing that recording! Because I know that, though my message may indeed come to Evan Seyfried's voice mail, it will most likely languish there, unanswered, for the next hundred years. Evan was never the master communicator even when he lived at home. He doled out tiny morsels of information about school and social life strictly on a need to know basis—and most of the time he figured we didn't need to know it. If a two year old could be described as the strong, silent type, well, that was Evan. At 22 the description is still rather apt. The Navy's secrets are safe with our son.

Sheridan is better, but not a whole lot better. Unlike Evan, he's not a complete phonaphobe. But he likes to call at night, preferably after I've been asleep about three hours, eager to settle in for a nice chat. While I may struggle to consciousness long enough to talk with him, I rarely remember anything we said the next morning. His is the wacky world of the young New Yorker about town, for whom "day" and "night" are mere suggestions. My bedtime has become embarrassingly early, so we are quite out-of-sync.

It's cliché to observe that Rosie is a relatively good correspondent because she's a girl, but whatever the reason, we actually do hear from her with more regularity. What Rose does, though, is specialize in The Cliffhanger—the frantic phone call about the super-urgent matter. After we've talked with her, we stew and stew and finally call her back to find out what's going on. At this point everything is, usually happily, resolved and she seems a tad bewildered that we're following up at all.

On the home front, PJ is a faithful phoner; that is, every afternoon when it's time for a ride home from football. Only Jules calls merely to gab, truly my mother Joanie's granddaughter.

I am somewhat more successful reaching my children via email, but am guilty of writing missives of such length that my recipients give up on being able to appropriately respond. So they often don't. Texting works better still; alas, I text the way I play sports: very slowly and very poorly. I threaten to join Facebook; so far it's just an idle threat, but one of these days…

It is a primal need of parents to communicate with their children, any way that works. And hearing back, however delayed the response, is a moment of the greatest joy. We know the kids are busy with life; we understand; we are patient (most of the time, anyway). It's just that we miss them, and love them so much.

And we are God's children. And He yearns to communicate with us, any way that works. And He waits, patiently (all of the time) as we stay so busy with life. He understands. But He misses us, and loves us so much.

A prayer is a voice mail, an email, a text message to Him. Whenever and however it is uttered, a prayer to our Parent is heard and cherished. Whether it be a one-or-two worder ("help" comes to mind), a late late night conversation, a cliffhanger, or just a request for a safe journey home, He is all ears. When we worry about finding the right time, place or words, we delay our response to the boundless love that is His daily gift to us. We need to relax about form and phraseology and just go for it.

And who knows? The habit of prayer may make gabbers of us all.

He's waiting to hear. Anytime is fine. Go on, drop Him a line.

POLAROIDS AND PRAYERS

"God has given us our memories that we might have roses in December."

--J.M. Barrie

My childhood was primarily, and very irregularly, documented with my Dad's Polaroid camera. As we moved from place to place, our small trove of dog-eared photographs shrank, thanks to our clever filing system of throwing them all in dresser drawers. Most of them are still probably stuck to the inside of a United Van Lines truck somewhere.

Last week, I took a two day break away after Christmas to spend time with my sister Carolyn, who has recently moved to the Delaware shore. One evening, as we sat up talking, she brought out a large box. "Whenever I could find these, I tucked them away so they would be safe," she said. When she opened it, C reopened our childhood. What an incredible surprise!

There they were, many of the old photos. My First Communion day. My late sister Maureen at age three, looking exasperated as she opens her ice cream cup to find chocolate, not her beloved vanilla. All three of us small girls at Normandy Beach, New Jersey. My Nana Cunningham playing the grand piano in her New York City living room. Though none of these pictures would ever win a photography prize, their power floored me. Looking at them, I was seven again, enduring the scratchy Communion veil, afraid of choking on the big dry Eucharist. There was fussy little Mo (besides vanilla ice cream, there wasn't much she <u>would</u> eat in those days). There was tiny C, "our" baby, grinning widely in her playpen on the porch. I could smell the clean salt air, so different from the noxious fumes of Manhattan; hear the sweet sounds of Strauss and Chopin as Nana's fingers flew over the keys…the torn, faded black and white photos unlocked a world again for me.

C is scanning them so we'll each have copies. Together, she and I are going to make scrapbooks this winter, as gifts for ourselves and, someday, for my own children. It only takes a few photos to bring back a day, a season, a whole stage of life. But those special few are treasures indeed.

As I sit at my desk at church, I love to look at the pictures of my church family, arranged on bulletin boards. I see the seventh graders making sandcastles on the beach. The beaming Confirmation class stands together on their special day. High schoolers pause to pose on their Appalachian Trail hike; a Service Saturday work crew smiles from a West Philadelphia schoolyard. Soon, my church kids will help me make a scrapbook too.

Some chilly day this winter, I invite you to revisit the long-ago and faraway lands of your old photographs. If you are a tidy saver, open the album pages and share some stories with folks you love. If you're like my family, open that dresser drawer and pull out the jumbled mass of snapshots. Treat yourself to a scrapbook, and write your story in pictures. Arrange in the pages the images of your nearest and dearest faces; and the faces you miss the most. Keep them where you can look at them often. And whenever you look at them, pray for them. Give them into God's care, over and over again. You can be sure He treasures them all, as much as you do.

In God's time, the baby sister who grins on a porch in 1962 is still there, somehow, held in the Divine embrace that holds that very same, all-grown-up sister today. Inside, in some mysterious way, we are all still every photo ever taken of us. Which makes those precious pictures bittersweet. And beautiful. And even, holy.

God bless you now, and then, and always.

A BLOOMING SHAME

"And the Lord God planted a garden in Eden, in the
east; and there he put the man whom he had formed."

--Genesis 2:8

Oh no. Spring again. How embarrassing.

Our neighborhood is filled with carefully mown lawns and
meticulously tended gardens, erupting in a riot of color and fragrance,
virtually our own branch of the Philadelphia Flower Show.

And then there's our house.

We purchased a home whose former owners were gardeners of
such talent that even in the Wonderful Land of Oz that is East Oreland
in springtime, ours was known as "the house with the beautiful yard."

For about two months.

At the end of that time we had pretty well polished off the delicate
blossoms and started destroying the hardier plantings. Our mimosa
sprouted fungus, our daffodils drooped and our tulips tanked. Ivy crept
over the flower beds. Then we killed the ivy. Our grass promptly took
the cue and died too. The little birdies skipped our perches in disdain.
Even the squirrels, not known as the pickiest creatures in the animal
kingdom, seemed to give the exterior of our abode a wide berth.

And things have only gone downhill from there. Other yards evoke the meadows of Provence, or the pristine flower gardens of the English countryside. Our yard tends to evoke downtown Death Valley.

It doesn't look like we even try, but actually we do (or at least Steve does). We mow, we prune, we weed (or at least Steve does). My forays into the great outdoors tend to just cut a wide swath of destruction, so I try to stay away. Still, the yard seems to know, somehow, that someone with the black thumb of doom lives nearby. The dandelions and gout weed know who's in charge. They are.

I don't get it. I love flowers as much as the next person. I would never deliberately commit planticide, and yet, spring after spring, I do. You have possibly read of my prowess with pets; I bat .000 in that department too. Indeed, it seems the only thing I can raise is children.

Sometimes I think of our yard as a metaphor for life (well, it's not good for much of anything else!) We are given a Paradise to enjoy, a riot of color and fragrance, of peace and harmony. And what do we do? We barrel through, stepping on the flowers, tearing up the trees, destroying everything in our path. We may be able to keep a semblance of order on our front lawn, but if you just take a peek in the back there is rot, there is ruin. And we don't mean to, we would never deliberately make such a mess of things. But we do.

We have a Gardener who is available to us 24/7, a Gardener who can help us rake up the moldy leaves and feed the parched grass, who can free the flowers from their bed of choking weeds. A Gardener who can help us make a Paradise again. And we don't even call Him. And so on we struggle, black thumbs against His green one.

But there is, always, a spring. And with spring, hope for another chance. With the Gardener by our side, we can wrest beauty out of the most colossal mess. The sun is a little brighter, a little warmer, every day now. While there is life, we can still learn. There's still time to make our gardens grow.

The Yard of the Month Award may be absolutely out of the Seyfrieds' reach. But this year, if we really try, we just may have a shot at Most Improved.

UNDER THE WEATHER

"I assume that to prevent illness in later life, you
should never have been born at all."

--George Bernard Shaw

I note, as our children progress from growing up to all grown up, there
is a marked difference in how we celebrate holidays. We no longer
throw up, as a rule. Our eardrums do not rupture. We do not break out
in festive spots. When the five kids were tiny, that was as much a part
of special days as fireworks and Yule logs: the ill-timed illness. The
New Year we toasted with Robitussin. The Thanksgiving when the
temperature of the roasting children rivaled the temperature of the
roasted turkey. The Memorial Day memorialized as the Chicken Pox
Wedding. Pop an Advil with me, won't you, as we stroll down memory
lane?

My own holiday health report growing up was none too good (like
the four New Year's Eves in a row that I had strep throat), so I
shouldn't have been too surprised. But, like most new moms, I entered
maternity confident that my offspring would be Superbabies, the
hardiest of stock. After all, staying healthy was a simple matter of
proper diet, fresh air and good hygiene, right? I nursed, I took them on
brisk walks, I scrubbed my hands till they were raw. Results? Sheridan

was in the ER with bronchitis over Fourth of July weekend. Evan endured a nasty bout of rotavirus, landing in Abington Hospital (week before Easter). Rosie had colic (Christmas), PJ had a whopping double ear infection (Halloween), Julie ended up in Abington with RSV, respiratory synticial virus (New Year's week). Seems my sickness track record trumped all my precautions after all.

For sheer drama, though, none of the array of childhood illnesses equaled the quadrifecta, the Chicken Pox Wedding. It was Memorial Day weekend, 1993. We were invited to our niece's wedding in Kansas City. More than invited, involved. Evan was ringbearer; Rose was flower girl. At that point in parenthood, we were so starved for fun and frolic that the prospect of a flight to Kansas with four kids under age six rivaled a Club Med vacay.

So, naturally, Evan came home festooned with red dots, three weeks before the Big Day. After diagnosis, our pediatrician prescribed Aveeno baths and a calendar...if we could make it past day 21 we were home free; the rest of the kids would most likely emerge from this bout of the pox unscathed.

Wedding Day minus one. Wedding rehearsal. Evan, a little scabby but otherwise adorable in his tiny tux. Rose, clear-skinned and cute in her flower girl regalia. Out of the woods, nearly!!

Carrie's Wedding Day! Sunny skies, happy guests, radiant bride. Evan does not lose the rings. Rosie does not lose her cool. The couple is united. It is a spotless moment in time.

Wedding Day plus one. We are relaxing in my sister-in-law's home, watching the Indianapolis 500 on TV (this is a family from Indiana, so the 500 is sacred ground), anticipating a couple of days R&R in Kansas City. Sheridan queries, "What's this red thing on my ear?" Simultaneously, Rose pipes up, "I have one of dose on my face!" PJ just squirms and scratches a red thing on his nose. We call Delta Airlines, pronto. Can we make it on board before a major breakout and our sure quarantine? Turns out we can, barely. Our voyage home is a tense affair, tenser still because we can't seem to get Rosie to quiet down ("Hey, Mom, here's annuder pox!! And I see annuder pox!!")

Home, to two weeks of more Aveeno baths and misery. Annuder holiday bites the dust.

I realize, with humble gratitude, that our parade of woes pales in comparison to families who battle truly serious illnesses. We have been lucky indeed to endure merely the usual aches and pains. But it has been sort of comical to note that many of our under-the-weather times coincide with "special" times on the calendar.

We live in this suspension, don't we? Happy/unhappy, good news/bad news? When all around us are dancing, how often are we in the doldrums? It can feel as if we live out of sync with the world.

But we are never alone. We have a God who is there through the happy and unhappy equally, the healthy and sick alike, the good news/bad news all the same. Out of sync with the world, we still live in sync with the One who made us and cares for us through it all. Who clears up those ear infections and tummy wobbles, in His time. Irrespective of the assigned dates of man-made festivity, our bodies travel through life, sometimes well, sometimes ill. All times loved.

So this year we will probably not mark the holidays with Benadryl and humidifiers. But we will always remember the baby years when we did, when we shepherded our little ones past the shoals of those first small calamities. And we will marvel at, and give thanks for, the healthy young adults our kids have become.

Happy, pox-free holidays. God bless us, everyone.

AFTER THE CURTIS CONCERTS

"The only proof he needed for the existence of God was music."

--Kurt Vonnegut

On several occasions recently, I had the opportunity to hear world premiere performances of new classical music at the Curtis Institute of Music. The works, composed by the six young student composers (including my Sheridan), were challenging, engaging, interesting and, often, beautiful. The audiences applauded these new additions to the classical repertoire, and the young men who wrote them took well-deserved bows.

These pieces of music, which together consumed hundreds and hundreds of hours of painstaking effort, imagination and inspiration supplemented with grueling "grunt work," tens of thousands of notes written, re-written, and divided into different instrumental parts...these pieces of music will, very likely, never be performed again. In a current climate where pop music reigns, the audience for classical music hovers around 2% of all concert-goers, and the audience for post-Beethoven works is less than half of that. The likelihood of any of these kids becoming household words in any but their own households is quite, quite small.

So, what drives them? There are surer roads to riches--just cross over to rock. Why do they pour their souls into expressive musical creations that will probably only reach a few ears? Their dedication flies in the face of our society's values, it would seem. But--just ask one of them. The answer will not involve a thirst for notoriety, a fat bank account (or even a steady income). The answer will likely include words like "passion," "commitment," "fulfillment," and "happiness." Most would say they <u>have</u> to compose--that only composing helps them reach what is deepest and truest in themselves. If they reach one person, touch one heart, with their music, they will be satisfied. Anything beyond that is a bonus. The very act of composing helps them to touch something eternal, something transcendent. And to talk with them, it is easy to catch their enthusiasm, and to be filled with hope for their future, and the future of classical music--changing in many respects, but with core values that remain the same.

In our current world, there are surely more popular things to be than followers of Jesus. And this is a pretty recent development. The world is filled with non-believers in Christ, some who never believed, some who espouse other faiths, some who were so badly burned by "Christianity" as it is often practiced that they stay far, far away from a church community. Recent statistics point to the United States as one of the top mission fields in the world, where millions have either never heard the Good News, or were subjected to a perverted version of Jesus' simple message of love and totally turned off. To stay committed, devoted, inspired when all around you are millions who don't, won't listen...is that crazy? Is there any point to being one of a small group when the world seems to have gone elsewhere?

We all need to answer this for ourselves. We need to look into our hearts and souls, and nurture the love-based relationship that brought us to faith in the first place. We need to worry less about other people's reaction, and concentrate on touching the transcendent in our lives. If we are fed spiritually by worshipping, praying, singing, volunteering, together as a Christian family, then we are in the right place for us. If we remain passionately committed, fulfilled, and happy in the love of Jesus, others (never mind the number) will notice. The world will be a better place, because we will act in such a way that the lot of mankind is improved. Force and intimidation will not convert. Grace, generosity and acceptance often will.

Rock music can be absolutely wonderful—edgy, bursting with energy and emotion, sometimes technically brilliant. This is rock's time on the throne of popular music. And, as rock waxes and wanes in the decades to come, classical music will still be written, still be played, still reach a deeply appreciative audience. Music is a sublime gift from God. Those who create music are truly blessed, and they bless others with their talent. John Cage or Audioslave? A matter of taste. We'll never all agree, but all of us can strive to live as our best selves, riding out the tides of popularity. We can live each day staying true to our own call.

Then, what may seem to some like cacophony, may become a glorious new harmony that rises to Heaven.

ST. NICHOLAS DAY AND OTHER DISASTERS

> "I give you a new commandment, that you love one another. Just as I have loved you, you also should love one another."
>
> --John 13:34

It was Sheridan's first holiday season. We manic first-time parents were determined to create a gingerbread and mistletoe wonderland for him: a Christmas filled with joy, with an array of enticing gifts under an ornament-laden tree. I well remember the shopping, the decorating, the dressing up. A shame Sheridan remembers none of this. Perhaps because he was seven months old. Still, if you look at any of the 38,000 photos we snapped that magical Yule, you'll see a hint of a twinkle in those baby eyes. Or perhaps it's tears of exhaustion and overstimulation. No matter!! We did Christmas right for him!

But wait—even before December 25th, there were other traditions to set in stone. My Irish background yields little in the way of special ethnic holiday treats, Guinness notwithstanding. So we plundered Steve's childhood for Jollie Olde German Customs.

And what did we find? December 6th! St. Nicholas Day, when little ones leave their shoes out to be filled with candy and small presents. How cute is that? A mini-run-up to Christmas Major! Steve recalled celebrating St. Nicholas Day with fondness, so we were off to the races. Now, Sheridan's tiny shoes at the time could only hold about two teething biscuits, so we decided to bring out the huge knitted stockings. These were, as the old song goes, both Deep and Wide. Legos, books, candy, oranges, nuts, matchbox cars, all sank to the bottom...it was a simple task to max out the Visa just on the stocking.

People with sense (as opposed to us) would have scrapped this one in Year Two. Instead, as our family grew, four more of the gargantuan stockings marched across the mantel, filled with what amounted to our retirement funds. What's worse, every single darned December 5th, right about 8 PM, I remembered that I hadn't yet shopped for SND. So after the little cherubs were in bed, it was off to the stores and a joyless search for enough odds and ends to feed the stocking monsters. By the way, I last did this exactly one year ago, and you can be sure I will do it again this December 5th. It is, after all, a tradition.

Another Jollie Olde Custom courtesy of the elder Seyfrieds: oyster stew on Christmas Eve. Again, the 38,000 photos of our holiday table can testify that we sat before bowls filled with milk and slimy briny things. Which led to yet another holiday tradition: pouring the kids' oyster stew down the drain, as child after child found Seyfried Stew intriguing, perhaps, but a little hard to swallow. Finally wised up on that one, but it took awhile.

It would seem, then, that many of our most cherished family traditions are the disasters. Your family probably has these too—the Charlie Brown tree, the slightly pink turkey, the tangled lights and frazzled tempers. And what is it we cherish about them? What makes the kids, hidebound traditionalists that they are, hold us to repeating these catastrophes year after year?

Maybe the real tradition is the laughter at grand plans gone awry, again. Airbrushed perfection is not, after all, very funny. Maybe the real tradition is the cockeyed and misplaced effort to create magic just because we love each other so much. Just maybe, when the holidays arrive and we are at our most fragile, most stressed, most vulnerable— maybe that is where we are most open to our deepest and truest feelings. And it may also be that when we open our flawed and misguided and foolish selves to someone we love, we stumble onto the true meaning of this season after all.

Hold each other close. Merry Christmas.

NERVOUS

"And can any of you by worrying add a single hour to your span of life?"

--Matthew 6:27

Yeah, yeah, I know it's true. In fact, I am sure I have subtracted probably 10 or 15 years from my earthly span with my endless fretting. But does this awareness stop me?

Hardly.

Take last Thursday, for example.

It was a New York City adventure involving two of our children, oldest and youngest. Sheridan was set to perform a piece he composed in a concert; Julie was set to take the bus, solo, from Manhattan to Boston to visit Rosie. What a perfect opportunity for Mom to swing into super-stress mode!!

All the way from Philly to New York, Julie chatted excitedly. She literally couldn't wait for this sisters weekend, and was even looking forward to the Bolt Bus that would ferry her, direct, from one city to the other. Meanwhile, I had conjured up quite the image of this bus—a dirty, unreliable wreck on wheels. Oh, and the passengers! A shady, seedy assortment right out of Dante's *Inferno*. What could I possibly have been thinking, giving the green light to this disastrous journey?

So of course the bus proved to be shining clean and spanking new. And her fellow travelers? A bunch of college students right out of a Gap commercial. My worry-meter, then, logically shifted to an image of her arriving in Massachusetts alone, with Rosie inexplicably delayed for their meeting. And sure enough, at 10 PM I got a frantic phone call: "Mom, she's not here. What am I going to do?" I knew it! I knew this would happen! But I didn't even have a chance to voice my panic before Julie continued, laughing, "Just kidding, Mom. Of course she picked me up on time. We're at her apartment now! You have GOT to stop worrying so much!"

At this, I relaxed slightly…but only slightly. My arms and legs were still numb from having been twisted into one rigid position for the entire 20 minutes of Sher's piano sonata earlier in the evening. This is my traditional way of "enjoying" his concerts—moving not a muscle, scarcely breathing, the only physical activity the profuse sweating of my palms. I always joke that I serve as Sheridan's "nerve sponge": my sheer white-knuckled terror is the X factor that makes his cool, calm and collected musical performances possible. But, I'm mortified to admit, I'm not really joking.

And in this current, very worrisome time, I know I have company. Many of us feel that our obsessing over the current financial crisis is somehow making a difference, besides the difference to our sleep, digestion and sense of balance. We have all the worst-case scenarios memorized, and we are the nerve sponges for the world.

But Jesus says NOT to worry, doesn't He?

Jesus says that Julie needs to live her life, to go ahead and take that Bolt Bus, and that He, along with Rose, will be there for the pick-up. Jesus says that the concert will go well because Sheridan has prepared, and not because his mother is sufficiently tense. And Jesus says that He is with us always, which would include our times of anxiety, loss and fear.

Of course, there are appropriate actions we can take, and He does not expect us to do nothing. But if we can just stop panicking, we can open ourselves to a great, great gift: "the serenity to accept the things we cannot change" right now. A serenity that can calm the world just when it most needs calming. A serenity that comes from our companionship with our Lord, who is here now and will be with us, rejoicing, when better times come.

Who will always be on the other end of our bus line, there for the pick-up.

THE FAITH OF A PLEBE

"…For truly I tell you, if you have faith the size of a mustard seed, you will say to this mountain, "Move from here to there", and it will move; and nothing will be impossible for you."

--Matthew 17:20

Our long wait was over. After a separation that began June 30th, on a mid-August weekend we were finally reunited with our "plebe", US Naval Academy Midshipman 4th Class Evan Seyfried. Parents Weekend was a most welcome chance to visit, to take Evan off the Academy grounds (the "Yard") for his first liberty, to hear stories of his incredibly challenging summer.

We were surrounded by other families, equally thrilled to see their sons and daughters, equally amazed at the transformations. Casual amblers had become brisk and purposeful walkers; "relaxed" housekeepers had become experts on cleaning supplies and techniques; kids who couldn't remember last night's dinner back home, now could recite the King Hall daily menu verbatim.

I couldn't help but notice the parallels between Evan's experience and the Christian life.

The Navy's core values of honor, courage and commitment are the engines that drive the Academy. The Naval officer is held to a high standard, and is expected to hold himself to an even higher one. Over four carefully planned years, the students are expected to push themselves to new levels of physical, mental and moral development each day, so that after commissioning they are prepared to lead others, and to serve their country—that is the ultimate goal.

The Christian life is also a challenge to be persons of honor, courage and commitment. Grateful for the ultimate gift we have been given as children of God, we show that gratitude by being good caretakers of our minds, our bodies and our souls. We strive to make solid moral choices every day, to lead by example, and to serve others before ourselves.

The plebe's journey begins on Induction Day, a day that begins all too early. Over a thousand teenagers are outfitted in whites, the boys' heads are shaved, and they plunge right into their rigorous training. That evening, they stand in Tecumseh Court and take the Oath of Office, thus enlisting in the US Navy. Looking at that sea of anxious and exhausted faces, it is clear that the Oath is a necessary, but only faintly understood, part of a very old ritual. Even so, that "I do" symbolizes the start of a very real commitment to an ideal, to something greater than themselves.

The Christian journey begins with Baptism. The baby, like the plebe, is garbed in white (and often bald!) He is blessed, and his sponsors make promises for him. He has committed to being part of something greater, to membership in the Kingdom of God. The baby doesn't understand—yet—but he will.

Six weeks after Induction Day, an utterly transformed group of young men and women gathers once again for a Reaffirmation Ceremony. Wearing dress whites, they salute sharply, stand proudly, having survived the crucible of Plebe Summer. Once more they are asked to take the same Oath of Office. This time, their "I do" is shouted, with much more confidence and conviction than before. They are beginning to learn what being a Naval officer is all about. They have surprised themselves with the limits they have already overcome. As parents, we are deeply touched, and look ahead to the time four years from now, when that same Oath will mean still more to these fine young people, because of the way they have lived.

The Christian formation that takes place through childhood, both at church and at home, is another kind of crucible. Through study, through nurturing, through example and, yes, through trial, children learn how to live a life of value. They come to respect themselves, and to respect others. They learn to make good choices, and so they grow in their faith as they grow physically.

On Confirmation Day, young people stand before their church family and reaffirm their Baptism. They are in their Sunday best. They stand proudly, confidently. This time, they can speak, and think, for themselves. This time, they have come to some understanding of what those words, those promises mean. And as they continue on this journey (which is, after all, lifelong), their lives will mean more and more as they strive to walk with Christ.

The rewards of a life bathed in the love of God are incalculable. This journey is well worth taking. But we all have to start somewhere. A life of faith begins with the first small step. It begins with the faith of a plebe.

A SLIGHT CHANGE OF PLANS

"A good traveler has no fixed plans and is not intent on arriving."

--Lao Tzu

From the very beginning, this was to be a summer of traveling for our family—Costa Rica and New Hampshire mission trips, PJ to Atlanta to visit friends, Evan doing summer training in Florida, all culminating in Rose's long journey to Thailand. Every excursion was planned, calendars were marked—in short, if you'd asked me in early June about our itineraries you would have gotten quite an earful of precise schedules and exact dates.

Suddenly everything changed. I found myself traveling roundtrip, and more or less constantly, from Lewes to Wilmington, Delaware and back. Instead of joining the mission trip crew heading up to Workcamp in Hollis, New Hampshire, my road led to a nursing home 90 miles from the town where we live and work during the summer.

It was a very different (and difficult) kind of mission, on a road I would never have chosen to take. But it was also an extraordinary journey.

My mom fell and broke her hip, just days after we had arrived in Lewes together, and just days before the New Hampshire trip was to begin. Mom was very ill, frightened, and in terrible pain. Clearly I could not leave her. We had a phenomenal team of adult leaders lined up to travel with our youth to New England, but I was the only woman, and Workcamp rules required at least one female chaperone. What in the world could be done?

Where my plans fell apart, God created a space for grace: the perfect person for the Hollis trip appeared, literally out of the blue. My friend Marge Keeley called to ask if we needed more help, having no idea about my mom's accident just the night before. And so a terrific person (with carpentry and painting skills, no less—believe me, I would have been no asset in that department!) was suddenly available to make the trip in my place.

All during that week—and the three weeks that followed—my family wore a path to the hospital, and after that to the rehab center, where Mom struggled to get back on her feet. The road held no attractions, unless you count the always hair-raising thrill of merging across four lanes onto Rt. 95 at Highway One. At times we were so tired we'd forget if we'd passed the midpoint of Dover yet, or if it was still 10 minutes ahead. It was frustrating to leave Mom each day, hoping she'd have a restful night, aware that she was pushing herself through so much discomfort to walk again, wondering when she'd be able to come home.

So why was it an extraordinary journey?

We traveled together. Sometimes I'd drive up with Sheridan, sometimes with Rose or Julie; Steve, my sister C and her husband took many a turn as well. At a time in our lives when there's been so <u>little</u> time to talk and really share our thoughts and feelings, we had the unexpected gift of three hours a day to be together, to laugh, and have some pretty deep discussions as well.

And we had the gift of time with Mom, to cheer her on as her great team of therapists helped her to reach each milestone—standing, walking down a hall again, starting to regain her lost mobility. And we had the chance to show her that the family she loves so much, loves her too.

God knew what the summer of 2005 would bring—we only thought we did. God knows what the year ahead will bring for all of us—we only think we do. In all of our journeys, planned and unplanned, God will be our traveling companion. And God will send us miracles, if we just learn how to see them. Even on Highway One.

JOYFUL COOKING

"I can't cook. I use a smoke alarm as a timer."

--Carol Siskind

My joy of cooking finally gave out.

Well, not my joy of cooking, but my first copy of *The Joy of Cooking*: the tattered, torn, gravy-splattered Bible of the kitchen. It owed me nothing. After all, I had used it nearly 40 years.

I remember the day I got it, as, of all things, a 10th birthday present. For the record, my other gifts that year were a Polaroid Swinger camera, bright orange fishnet stockings and a very "mod" newsboy cap. Ah, the sixties!

While the other presents came and went, *Joy* became a cherished friend to this budding chef. I was fascinated by all things culinary, even as a preteen. This is not because I learned the secret of flaky pastry from Mom, or a smooth Hollandaise from Grandma. Au contraire. I come from a line of truly horrendous cooks.

When I was little our family lived in New York City. Nana and Pop Cunningham (Dad's folks) lived just a few blocks away. Every Monday and Thursday Nana would pick me and my sister Maureen up from school and bring us back for dinner at their apartment. That gave Mom a break, and time alone with baby Carolyn. We loved spending evenings with Nana, who spoiled us silly. But dinner at Nana's was, shall we say, an experience. It generally involved "roast" (roast what, we were never quite sure). It arrived on the table still rolled and wrapped in butcher's twine, charred beyond recognition. Several times we ate some of the twine, unable to distinguish it from the meat. Pop was her perfect "other," as he had the original cast iron stomach. Indeed, Pop was partial to breakfasts of cold canned baked beans, strawberry ice cream and four or five cigars. They were quite a match.

On the home front things were not much rosier. Mom was a militant non-baker, and the TV dinner queen. Vegetables were what you ate on Thanksgiving, if Mom remembered to open the cans. It was, I imagine, with relief that Mom bought the cookbook, and turned the oven over to me.

It was a new day in the Cunningham kitchen. Armed with *Joy,* I started producing beef Wellington, asparagus amandine and chocolate soufflé. I wasn't really interested in learning scrambled eggs or meat loaf, so typical weeknight dinners ran to Coq au Vin and Veal Orloff. Our grocery bill climbed; we all put on weight. But I discovered a love for preparing food that has never left me.

I wish I could say my kids learned flaky pastry and smooth Hollandaise at my knee, but, I confess, I am a kitchen control freak. My secret recipes remain secrets. The boys can cook respectably now, but no thanks to me. How Rosie ended up learning to bake so well is a small miracle.

As I sent *The Joy of Cooking* to the big bookstore in the sky, I found myself saying a little prayer:

Dear Lord,

> *Thank you for the gift of food, and the gift of delight in its preparation. Remind me to untie my apron strings, and give my family a chance to discover the fun of cooking for themselves. Remind me, too, that food is only a small part of dinner. We are fed, most importantly, by our loving relationship with those who share our meals. I hope, someday, my kids remember my pasta primavera, and me, even a fraction as fondly as I remember Nana's burned toast and Mom's mystery casseroles. And with a fraction of the love I*

feel when I think of these two horrendous cooks and wonderful, wonderful women. The joy of cooking is nothing compared to the joy I'll feel when I see them again in Your Kingdom.

Amen.

ANOTHER PIECE OF THE PUZZLE

"The whole conviction of my life now rests upon the belief that loneliness, far from being a rare and curious phenomenon, peculiar to myself and to a few other solitary men, is the central and inevitable fact of human existence."

--Thomas Wolfe

The other day I came across a dog-eared piece of paper, with a couple of paragraphs scribbled in pencil. It was the message I gave at my dad's funeral, 11 years ago this April. He lived one week after a massive stroke, and I had taken my four children (I was newly pregnant with Julie) and traveled to Atlanta to be there for those last days. He never really regained consciousness, so any conversation in the hospital room was one-sided.

I had made the same hurried trip south 24 years ago, after my sister Maureen's fatal car accident. Another shock, another parting with no real goodbye. But there was a huge difference. Mo was my Irish twin— we were 11 months apart. We had shared so much, from clothes to confidences, from laughter to tears, that, in the end, it didn't really feel anything was left unsaid, young as she was at her death. We knew how very much we loved each other.

Dad and I had a…tricky relationship, let's say. At various times during my childhood and youth, it didn't feel much like a relationship at all. We shared no confidences. He seemed very detached from all of our lives. I always jumped to the conclusion that he disliked me, and I felt alternately angry and guilty. Dad died with just about everything between us unresolved.

And so, an odd eulogy from his oldest daughter. Instead of the outpouring of warm and funny anecdotes and sweet memories one might expect at a time like this, this is in fact part of what I wrote:

If it is true that each of us is a puzzle, made up of many pieces, my father, Tom Cunningham, was the most challenging puzzle I ever knew. Each of us in this church—

his wife, his daughters, his grandchildren—knew a few parts of Dad, but no one could ever really fit the puzzle together, probably not even Daddy himself. He was an intensely private, quiet man, a man who seemed alone even in the middle of a crowded room, or in the heart of his family…

It was an honest message. He was such a mystery to me.

But here's the strange part.

Our relationship hasn't ended. It is still growing. And, slowly, the mystery is clearing up.

In the years that have passed, I find myself thinking of him more and more. As I wrestle with the difficulties of life in middle age, I have come to understand that life got the better of Dad, from early on, and that there really was no malice or lack of caring in his attitude towards me or my sisters. It is not damning with faint praise to say "he did the best he could." I have come to believe that he really did. And that we all have our limitations. And that we all have our communications problems. And that we all are puzzles to ourselves at times.

My younger kids have vague memories of Dad, if any. They have said they feel sad that they never knew him. Many times I could have replied, "Don't worry. Neither did I." But that is no longer true. Now, I often feel his presence. There are moments my selfish longing for what he couldn't give me on earth begins to give way to something better. Something that feels like tenderness. Something that feels like love.

And so we travel on, together, Dad just out of sight, in a Heaven that may be much closer than I could have dreamed of.

LEARNING TO BE DRIVEN

"For surely I know the plans I have for you, says the Lord, plans for your welfare and not for harm, to give you a future with hope."

--Jeremiah 29:11

Now it is Rose's turn. Her 16th birthday has arrived, and with it the slip of paper that spells "freedom"—or at least, freedom-in-training. My daughter has her learner's permit. It's time for me to get into the car on the passenger side. Oh, I can show her the windshield wipers, point out the emergency flashers, and set her on the road, but the keys are in her hand, now. And she's taken to it very quickly. In no time at all, she will be venturing out, beyond the neighborhood, onto expressways, snaking through rush hour city traffic, tearing across the country on insane late night whirlwind adventures, ignoring posted speed limits, failing to yield, tailgating, drag racing…

Excuse me. I got carried away there. Actually, I have no doubt that Rosie will soon be an excellent driver, skillful, law abiding and responsible. Rose will, in fact, be a much better driver than her mother.

The problem is not Rose learning to drive. It's me learning to be driven.

You see, I have a teensy little problem with control. I confess that hearing people say "How <u>can</u> you do as much as you do every day?" is music to my ears. Well, the truth is, I deserve no credit for my energy level. And while I seem to keep quite a few plates in the air, I drop more than I'd ever let you know. Hard work is a good thing. Addiction to an image of being the hardest worker, is not. Learning to let go of the reins, to hand over the car keys, is more than a lesson in humility. It is a gift to those wonderfully competent others I've been shortchanging every time I insist on being in charge.

There are those who struggle with helplessness, who fear taking charge of anything. For them, life's journey often takes them to the scary but amazing place where they have to learn just how much they <u>can</u> do. For others of us, the road leads to an equally scary, equally amazing place. Here, it is all right to let things go sometimes. Here, we learn how to gracefully, and gratefully, receive. I'm not there yet, but hopefully I'm getting closer.

I'm getting used to being a passenger these days, wonder of wonders. And I am learning to be glad to have my daughter as my driver.

ADVENTURES IN MISSING THE MARK

"Shallow understanding from people of good will is more frustrating than absolute misunderstanding from people of ill will."

--Martin Luther King, Jr.

A glimpse of Seyfried birthdays past...

Evan is 2! Winnie the Pooh party!

Aunt C creates beautiful and detailed Winnie the Pooh piñata

Guests arrive

None of Evan's friends want to hit piñata, as no one wants to hurt Pooh Bear

Finally Dad whacks Winnie, candy spills out, children cry

PJ is 6! Surprise Party One!

Send birthday child out with Dad to "go to the Acme";
guests arrive and hide

Birthday child returns home

Guests leap out from their hiding places

Birthday child is completely and utterly…

Unsurprised, acting as if hiding and leaping friends
happen every day

Rose is 8! Fancy Dinner Party!

Hire Sheridan to play violin; set table with best
tablecloth and candles

Guests arrive, hoping for pizza and a video

No one listens to Sheridan's music

No one eats the fancy dinner

Steve is 40! Surprise Party Two!

Send Steve to bring gas can to "stranded" out-of-gas
friend in Bucks County

Guests begin to arrive, parking around the block to be
stealthy

Steve returns home, 30 minutes early, having found
nifty shortcut to stranded friend

Guests continue to gradually arrive and "surprise"
guest of honor

Each and every time I planned one of these birthday parties I forgot
one tiny but important detail. Such as: two year olds hate beating up
Winnie the Pooh; it is impossible to surprise a six year old; eight year
olds usually don't adore beef stroganoff; 40 year olds (at least my 40
year old) tend to be pretty good at reading maps. I meant well, I always

meant well—and tried hard. But something was always just a little off, just missing the mark.

And this is exactly why serving others can be so tricky. We persist in making small talk with the homeless man in the soup kitchen; he evades our eyes. We descend on an Indian reservation to help, and are met with cold stares. We nervously blurt out "get well soon" to the hospice patient. We mean well, we always mean well—and try hard. But we need to stop and think. Have we forgotten some pretty important details? How would we feel if we were homeless—maybe embarrassed? If we were Native Americans on the reservation, maybe proud? If we were dying patients, maybe ready to stop pretending? And by the way, I've done every single thing I've just described.

Jesus looked at—really penetrated the souls of—everyone he helped, everyone he healed. His interactions with people were very personal and thoughtful. He took each person's unique situation into account, and was able to make a powerful connection every single time.

Can we try to follow in His footsteps? We can't always hit the bull's eye, of course. Into each life a piñata must fall. But when we stop and think, and then walk that mile in other shoes, we can make an incredible difference in the world. By really looking, listening, and meeting people right where they are, not where we think they should be.

And that might well bring us, all of us, just a little closer to the mark.

FALLEN LOGS AND FISHING BOOTS

"I search for the realness, the real feeling of a subject, all the texture around it...I always want to see the third dimension of something...I want to come alive with the object."

--Andrew Wyeth

If you are an art lover—or even an art liker—run, don't walk, to the current Andrew Wyeth exhibition at the Philadelphia Museum of Art. It is an extraordinary collection of works by one of America's premiere artists, who at age 89 still lives and paints in his hometown of Chadds Ford. Best known for the painting *Christina's World*, Wyeth takes the viewer deeply into HIS world, a world where man and nature are intricately intertwined. It is a world where ordinary objects become profoundly symbolic, where monumental emotions of love and joy and loss are captured in a painting of an old bucket, an empty room, a tattered pair of fisherman's boots.

As I strolled through the galleries the other day, I was often moved to tears by the simplicity and beauty of Wyeth's vision, and awed by his mastery of technique. A painting of a young boy running, behind him a large hill, was lovely in itself. It took on much deeper meaning when I learned the boy was Wyeth himself, the hill was a symbol of his father, artist N.C. Wyeth, who had been killed at a railroad crossing. Andy mourned this loss so greatly, and for the rest of his life has painted the father he never had time to capture in a portrait, by painting his father as nature—a mighty hill, a large boulder. In a significant way, these "portraits" are more powerfully evocative of the essence of the elder Wyeth than a picture of his face would have been.

Another highlight was a series of studies for the famous painting *Groundhog Day*. Preliminary sketches indicate that there was a person in the kitchen sitting at the table, neighbor Karl Kuerner. Also in the scene was the Kuerner's dog. Outside the kitchen window was a stark landscape. As the studies developed, the man was eliminated. Then the dog was painted out, as Wyeth "looked" out the window and saw a rough-hewn cut log, part of which resembled canine teeth. The log, then, would represent the dog. And so the winnowing process continued until the final painting emerged—a simple kitchen table, with a place setting for one, a window looking out on a fallen log. The "ghosts" of Karl and his dog are palpable.

Wyeth is a master of reducing people to their core, the essence of their being. He does it by eliminating, by paring down, by erasing, by refining. I was struck by the relevance of this process to our own life's journey. So much of life is spent in accumulation—of education, of a house, a car, of material things. The danger is that we can hide in the clutter of our things, and totally mask our true selves, our essence. And so, difficult as it may be, there is great beauty, clarity and power in the process of shedding excess "things." We become more fully…us. The unique souls we were created to be.

As we open the windows at last and revel in the sun, in the return of the flowers in springtime, many of us will be moved to throw things out, to give things away. It just feels better to have less, to have breathing space in this clean and bright new season. As you sort through the objects that surround you, or as you gaze out your window at the natural world, what best symbolizes you? If Andrew Wyeth set out to capture your true self, what might he paint?

And if you don't know, isn't it time to think about it?

UNGIFTED

"The winds of grace are always blowing; all we need
to do is raise our sails."

--Anonymous

Just a few of the things I am ungifted at:

Bike riding. I have dined out on this tidbit for many a moon. I grew
up in Manhattan, where only kamikaze bicycle messengers brave the
mean streets. My little red trike didn't stand a chance. When I moved to
the burbs, I had reached the age of acute embarrassment, and didn't
dare try to ride. Hence: I am 52. I could not ride a bike if doing so
would save me from the Apocalypse.

Parallel parking. If I go somewhere—like, say, the city of
Philadelphia—

and there is a need to parallel park, I have a simple solution. I drive
home.

Blowing up balloons. Don't ask. Just totally creeps me out.

Saying good-bye. Ask my children, especially a) Evan, who is
shortly leaving for Hawaii for the next (sob) several years; b) Rosie,
whose regular jaunts to faraway spots always cause me great angst; c)
PJ, who recently left for Millersville University and, though he has left

traces of himself behind (can you say phone charger? Wallet? Contact lenses?) still has wrenched my heart with his departure.

And this, my friends, merely scratches the surface of my incompetence.

In several of his letters, Paul writes, famously, of spiritual gifts. Prophecy, Ministry, Exhortation, Discernment of Spirits, Healing, etc. These passages always make me feel almost cosmically inadequate. Spiritual gifts? I barely register on the radar screen. But sometimes, I read the lists, and I wonder: what teaches us the greater spiritual lessons? Our God-given strengths, or our equally God-given frailties?

I guess we all have Bible folk we identify with, some more than others. I am foursquare in the Peter camp. I often feel like a spiritual oaf, bumbling my way from day to day, rejecting what I'm supposed to be accepting, doubting when I'm supposed to be trusting. Wildly flawed.

So, what to make of us, the company of the inept? We may not be particularly spiritually gifted, but we have a couple of things going for us.

For one thing, the ungifted are usually fairly humble. It's not as if we have much of a choice. Watch me attempt to pedal uphill, or nearly blow my brains out trying to inflate a balloon, and you'll see that my dignity has pretty much left the building.

For another, the ungifted have a natural empathy for their fellow bozos. Put us in a room full of other ungifteds and we become the ultimate support system. Hey, anyone want to form a Chronic Solitaire Losers Club? I am so there.

Seriously, though, we live in a world designed to reward winners, and disdain the rest of us. We raise our children in a culture so sensitive to their sensitivity that we award trophies to every tiny soccer munchkin; we grade on a 5.0 scale. As we age, we airbrush and Botox and dye away our imperfections.

And we worship a God who radically, radically, rejects those values.

Hard as it may be to look in that mirror and face those myriad shortcomings, we don't gaze alone. Our Lord stands behind us, and beside us. He reassures us that we may not find ourselves sharing in the laundry list of spiritual gifts (Interpretation of Tongues, anyone?) He knows us to be far more Peter than Paul. Maybe our giftedness is—

stick with me now—our very ungiftedness. God can and does work through Mother Teresa and Elise Seyfried alike (though we are emphatically NOT alike). And God's power is made manifest through our misses, maybe even more than our hits.

The grace of God is a gift, an unearned, amazing gift. So who better to receive a gift than the ungifted? If it's been awhile since you've unwrapped the present of His love, it's time to party. There are definitely spiritual gifts, and most definitely those who, as my Grandma Berrigan would say, were standing behind the door when the Lord was giving out those spiritual gifts.

So come on out, come out from behind the door. It's safe. You klutzes, you goofballs, you each actually fit quite well with the Divine Plan. Unclench your hearts and open your hands to receive the everlasting gift of His grace.

MISSING ROSE

"And ever has it been that love knows not its own depth until the hour of separation."

--Kahlil Gibran

On January 4th, we're halfway through Rosie's year in Thailand (but who's counting, right?) While I am sure it is, for the most part, flying by for her, it's been a long five months here in Oreland. We would never, ever wish her to be anywhere but exactly where she is this year, having the exotic and amazing experience she has dreamed of her whole life. There are moments, however, when we might wish the "exotic and amazing" was not occurring 10,000 miles away.

Missing her today, I thought I'd write a bit about the presence of her...absence. From birth, Maureen Rose Seyfried has been a force to be reckoned with, and utterly one-of-a-kind. Newborn, she wailed so incessantly that the older boys finally came to me and queried, "Mom? You said we were going to love having a baby sister. When are we going to start loving her?" As a toddler, Rose quickly decided that playgroup meant the other children played, while she sat and chatted with the moms. From there she grew to be the independent spirit who always wore two different color socks—and read different books, and thought different thoughts. Her cookie baking business was but a means to an end, the end being financial freedom to travel—Jamaica, England, etc. When Rose was around things were louder, brighter, often rather too dramatic, but never, ever boring.

The spring and summer, during which we all focused on the journey ahead, were busy and happy months for her. If she was anxious about the language, the distance, the challenge, she rarely voiced it. Suddenly it was an August morning, and we stood in the Philadelphia airport, and the vague future possibility became the all-too-clear reality. She was taking off for Detroit, where she would meet up with other Rotary exchange students, then on to Tokyo, Bangkok and, finally, Chiang Rai. She joked with her siblings, and her dear friend Hannah, until it was the moment of separation. We all cried, hugged, and clung to her as she prepared to walk through security. Our tears and noise attracted the glances of other travelers in line. The tension was broken when Sheridan shouted, "Have a good time in Detroit!" and we watched people shake their heads at the family so overly bonded that seeing someone off to Michigan would cause such an outpouring of grief.

The days passed. I found at least three items she forgot to bring, and three more that I'd hoped to give her for the trip. School started. Julie wrote story after story in school about the sister she loved so much and missed so dearly. PJ moved into her room. Everyone started borrowing her CDs; I started borrowing her clothes. We all started quoting her around the house. A phone call was a rare event, and a cause for celebration. We thanked God daily for the inventor of the instant message. We mailed ridiculous packages to Chiang Rai, spending $90 to send candy and fashion magazines.

We knew she was changing—who couldn't be profoundly changed by the experience she was having? We hoped she wasn't changing too much. It struck us that we, too, would be different when she got home. PJ was getting so tall. Julie was playing travel basketball. Dad was doing some film acting. Mom was, at long last, beginning piano lessons. We wanted to freeze time so all would be as she'd left it, to ease her transition back to us, but of course we couldn't. In many ways, we will reconnect in June as new and different people.

Life is filled with permanent losses, and I rejoice that this one is temporary. But it is a loss, and we all feel it, every single day. And so 2006 begins as 2005 ended for the Seyfrieds. Missing Rose.

THE SPOILER

"Plenty of people miss their share of happiness, not because they never found it, but because they didn't stop to enjoy it."

--William Feather

So you can tell me. Go on. How does it end?

OK, I admit it. I have to know how everything turns out. It's a great comfort.

I started *Gone with the Wind* with "Frankly, my dear," and only then flipped back to page one. *Sophie's Choice* was known to me within five minutes of reading. I had to know the identity of Luke's father before I could enjoy *Star Wars* and believe me, it is all I can do to keep from opening *Harry Potter and the Deathly Hollows* first to page 759.

If I had my way as a parent, I would be able to use a magical machine to time travel ahead and just make sure my chickies would survive leaving the nest. I could handle a lot, a lot better, if I could just get a sneak peak at their adulthood.

And, while I'm in confessional mode here, I like to "pre-disaster" as well. This concept became famous in *The World According to Garp* when Garp purchased a house that a plane had just crashed into—the logic being that it was "pre-disastered," and henceforth would be perfectly safe. I plan for the plane crash. And the random can of paint toppling down on my head from a high ladder. And a fish bone to choke me at dinner. The more horrors my mind can conjure up, the more I feel protected from actual peril, which tends to arrive unanticipated, no?

As humans, I think we all badly want reassurance that things will turn out just fine. We pray for that elusive peace of heart, and some are lucky enough to attain it. For the rest of us, it's a constant struggle. Mind games aside, there is no such thing as a pre-disaster, and there is no handy-dandy device that enables us to flip to the last page of our story for a morale booster. Stuff happens, as the saying goes (more or less in those words), and a lot of that stuff we would never, ever choose—or be able to predict.

Since each moment, each day, each lifetime has such an element of surprise, it is pointless to imagine catastrophe. It is sad to be a spoiler, rushing to the conclusion of each adventure and missing the wonder of what should come first. There are some things in life we can control but so very much we cannot. Life should be a banquet to be savored, not a minefield to be navigated or a DVD to fast-forward.

Children seem to understand this, instinctively. The carefree kids of our Vacation Bible School, who didn't really worry a whole lot about what Wednesday's craft would be, or if the snack on Thursday would be their favorite. The kids of San Ramon, Costa Rica, who greeted us each day of our mission trip with hugs and happiness and hope. They all seem to know how to live in every second, really live. Not flip to page 759. Not wring hands and fret about far-flung possibilities.

Jesus knew that children had the key. He urged us all to become like them. He didn't promise a life without turmoil, the unexpected, or, yes, disaster. He counseled us to relax, to trust, to let our story unfold in its own time and way. He promised us Paradise, but not Paradise now. Meanwhile, there are so many gems to be uncovered on earth if we look, and look patiently. Moments of shining beauty and joy, right there amidst the tedium, the terror, the million unpredictables of everyday existence.

I know this. I do know this. Banquet, not minefield. To look at things otherwise is to be a spoiler, for myself.

So I take it back. Surprise me. Don't tell me how it ends. Oh, except maybe for *Harry Potter*. I promise to keep that quiet.

SIGHT UNSEEN

"For now we see in a mirror, dimly, but then we will see face to face. Now I know only in part; then I will know fully, even as I have been fully known."

--1 Corinthians 13:12

Good thing we have those nice big name tags here at church. Nowadays, you're all looking a little blurry to me. But if I look at just the right angle, I can still read your name tag! It has been gradually, then rapidly, becoming apparent that I am heading toward blind-as-a-bat-ness. Was it really three years ago on retreat that Pastor Mike pointed to a singular cow in a field as we drove by, and I replied, "I see them"? Ever since, the jocular banter has flowed about my status as one of the optically challenged. Last month, driving in an unfamiliar neighborhood on a dark, rainy night, I literally had to get out of the car twice to walk over to the street signs to read them. When I can read signs at all, I comically misinterpret them. In my hazy world, the convenience store advertises for "overweight cashiers,"and Hertz offers a great rate on "dental cats."

So what the heck is it that has kept me from the opthamologist? Vanity? Maybe, but I actually don't think that's the case here. I've always loved the look of attractive glasses. Laziness? More likely—

how ever will I find the time to get checked, get prescribed, get fitted? But that still doesn't tell the whole tale. In truth, there really is no plausible reason for my letting my vision slide to this degree. Me, who cries over beautiful sunsets (or did back in the days when I could see them)? Me, who loves to read almost more than anything else? And what's with me endangering other people as I grab those car keys and take off, in which direction I can't quite tell?

St. Paul writes, "For now we see in a mirror, dimly, but then we will see face to face. Now I know only in part; then I will know fully, even as I have been fully known."

I've been thinking of my vision, or lack thereof, lately in this context. There is a perfect Heaven, and it is not so very far out of sight. We are made with a longing to see it, to be in it. And yet we can't see it because we also long NOT to see it, to drift along in the fog, as it were. We see well enough to get by, most days. We cope. The effort of achieving greater clarity is just too much. Then there is the challenge that would face us if we really could see ourselves. Magnifying mirrors simultaneously fascinate and repel us, zooming in on our every flaw. Clear sight leads to beautiful things, but also requires some painful honesty.

While we dwell here on earth, that perfect Heaven will remain visible only in glimpses. But we can try every day to improve our vision, to look for signs of the divine in our lives, and to mirror the divine for those we contact. Imagine how much better our world would begin to look, to all of us.

So it's off to read that goofy eye chart. Strangely, I'll miss my myopia, I think. Miss the gentle blurring of the rough edges of life. But I do believe it's high time I began to see.

VINEYARD HEAVEN

"You can fall in love at first sight with a place as well as a person."

-- Alec Waugh

Well, we did it. We took our first "family vacation" in memory. Oh, we did one or two overnight trips over the years, but even by our flexible definition, one night does not a vacation make. To gather a critical mass of Seyfrieds in one place for R&R is a true rarity. We do go down to Rehoboth Beach, Delaware in the summers, but that is where we work, running our children's theatre. Leading workshops and performing day and night is not exactly the stuff of leisure.

Here's the story of how we ended up at the Quinns' gorgeous home on Martha's Vineyard. At last year's silent auction to benefit the Alaska mission trip, I jumped in early on the bidding for the house (Steve was out of the room). Thinking I'd "jump out" once things heated up, I put in a couple more bids and, lo and behold! Going, going, gone—to us. Just imagine Steve's initial surprise and delight when he heard about my little impulse purchase!

As time went by, however, it became clear that, whenever we could manage to get away, the time in Martha's Vineyard would be a great blessing for our gang. Enforced time off, time to reconnect in a relaxed way in a beautiful setting. Our upcoming trek seemed like an oasis in the dry and difficult desert that was the past year for us. Even when it became clear that we'd have to make plans without our Evan (the Naval Academy had a claim on him for most of May), it would still be well worth the effort to clear our schedules, pack and go.

Needless to say, we had a blast. The weather was unreal (for New England in May that is—85 and sunny). The house was cozy and comfortable. The island offered a wealth of activities—and we gave ourselves permission to do nothing sometimes too. Sheridan's girlfriend Quan was able to join us, which added so much to the fun. She's from China, and the trip was a series of firsts for her—first minigolf, first time skipping stones, etc. We will never forget Quan's delight in learning checkers and chess—or the revelation that our 12 year old Julie is quite the poker player! We hiked at Menemsha to enjoy a glorious sunset, hit the beach, ate constantly, and laughed even more than that.

When vacations are not part of your family routine, it's amazing how difficult they are to justify. And that's ridiculous, because batteries that are never recharged…well, you know. People who take a break every now and then return to their work refreshed, renewed and, yes, more productive than had they continued toiling away 24/7. God actually wasn't kidding about that day of rest. But many of us have decided that the world would in fact falter and fail without our constant and vigilant presence on the job.

Some of us need to learn that time off is indeed part of our Father's plan for us. He never intended for us to worry and work ourselves through every moment of our lives. For every one of us, there is a place that beckons, that encourages us to slow down and just be.

I hope this summer brings each one of you, wherever you go, your own games of checkers. Your own technicolor Menemsha sunset. Your own little Vineyard Heaven.

THE ANNIVERSARY WALTZ

"Love is an ideal thing, marriage a real thing."

-- Goethe

"The Anniversary Waltz." That was the name of a song my Mom sang often over the years as she drifted through the day. I don't remember all the lyrics, but some do come back...*So tell me I may always dance the Anniversary Waltz with you...Will this be the answer to our future years...with millions of smiles, and a few little tears?...* I remember thinking it sounded sad, kind of pleading. Definitely not a tone of confidence that this couple would still be together in those "future years." At that point my parents had been married maybe nine years (I was eight), and I couldn't help but think they'd probably had a good long run.

March 19, 2007, I will be married....30 years. I met Steve at 15, got engaged at 17 and married when I'd just turned 20.

Grand idea? Nah, not exactly. Every time one of my kids passes the magic 17 milestone without either sporting or giving a diamond ring, I breathe a huge sigh of relief. Steve and I were so very much more fortunate than we knew at the time. It's hard to imagine that same kind of lucky lightning striking again with one of our offspring. Teenagers aren't ready for this, this promise of a lifetime. They need to be studying, playing, traveling extensively, living as young adults for themselves before they sign on to live for someone else. But we'd been out of the room when that lesson was taught, I guess. And so in we plunged.

Random wedding memories:

I bought the most expensive dress I'd ever imagined wearing: $125. I vowed I'd wear it again. Yeah, right. But, with roses in my hair the overall effect was OK. It was the seventies, remember?

Armed with a budget of about zero, we hired a friend's friend to be the photographer. He did pretty well, some funky camera angles. I can't blame him for the frozen smiles on bride and groom—that's how we really looked that day…happy-ish, and plenty scared.

We hired a violinist with the Atlanta Symphony, a church member, to play a Ravel piece we loved, as a processional. As the bridesmaids started down the aisle, all I could hear was the organ accompaniment. The violinist had a sore back, it turned out, and just didn't show up. I tried not to think of this as an omen.

I told the priest (oh, the temerity) that he was NOT to say the part of the vows where I agree to cheerfully accept children. I had NO intention of having children. I didn't even LIKE children. He buckled, and the line was cut.

OK, you can stop laughing now. I mean it.

We honeymooned in New York, for five days. Two of them were spent driving the Chevy Vega back and forth from Atlanta to New York City. We saw three Broadway plays (went to the half-price ticket booth in Times Square), ate cheap, and arrived home with 57 cents. Whoopee.

Every married couple has its own goofy, painful, wonderful story. Every year is another chance to dress up and dance that Anniversary Waltz together. Every year is a chance to make it, indeed, the answer to their future years. Some dances are cut short, by death or divorce. Some are like dance marathons of the Depression, two exhausted people propping each other up.

But after 30 years, I know there is a reason why marriage is a sacred institution. God <u>blesses</u> us, the crazy people who take this plunge, who say no to so much, to say yes to one another. Who look at each other: graying, slightly pudgy, slightly creaky, and see beauty.

And, still, the one they promised to be there for. For nine years. For 30. Maybe even more.

Happy Anniversary, sweetheart. I've got my dancing shoes ready. Thank God.

WORKING

"Whatever your hand finds to do, do with your
might…"

--Ecclesiastes 9:10

Do you remember your first job? I know I certainly do.

At age 11, I began to babysit. My first customers were a family
with four children. I cared for their darlings for 35 cents an hour. (Note:
please don't contact me! My rates have gone up!) These were the little
charmers who, on my watch, fed their goldfish down the garbage
disposal. Other babysitting adventures included the parents who gave
me two pages of instructions regarding their beloved dog Snoopy. At
the end of this presentation they added offhandedly, "Oh, and the baby
will probably just sleep." Then there were the siblings who constantly
tormented each other. One actually grew up to be the place kicker for
the Chicago Bears. It figured. He'd had enough practice place-kicking
his brother.

> Later resumé highlights:
> Salesperson at an upscale Danish furniture store.
> During the entire time of my employment there, I made
> exactly two sales. Both to myself.

Hostess at Daddy's Money Restaurant in Atlanta. Yes, it really WAS as classy as it sounds.

Actress at nearly every small-time dinner theatre in the Southeast. Oh, it was a choice assortment: the Mountaineer in Hurricane, WV; the Barn in Nashville, TN; the Celebrity in Birmingham, AL. The Celebrity shared space with a bowling alley. During quiet moments of the play, the phrase "you could hear a pin drop" took on a whole new meaning.

Kelly Girl (an array of temporary jobs, which could also count as acting). I pretended to fit in at a hospital, a law firm, and a blue jean factory. I don't believe anyone was fooled for a minute, as I mispronounced, misdialed, misfiled and mislabeled my way through the days.

Everyone has their early employment stories, both entertaining and horrific. Steve recalls his first summer job in steamy Valdosta, GA, toiling away at Buster Basford's cardboard box company. Good times.

These first jobs provide invaluable lessons in responsibility. They offer opportunities to stretch in myriad ways, as we learn to do all sorts of things we never thought we could. We meet interesting people from all walks of life, and develop some unlikely friendships. We learn respect for workers everywhere, and gratitude for the paychecks we earn.

This summer, a record number of young people, including my PJ, are pounding the pavements, looking for the job that will help fund their dreams. You'll see them scooping ice cream, lifeguarding, bussing tables, doing yard work. And when you see them, maybe you'll remember your own stories. Maybe you'll give them an encouraging smile, or drop an extra dollar in the tip jar. Maybe you'll even say a little prayer for them.

And so we look forward to relaxing a bit in the months to come, thanking God for the gift of leisure time. But we can, and should, also give thanks to God for the gift of work, all kinds of work. The jobs we love and the jobs we merely endure. Each a chance to serve others and grow to be more well-rounded, wiser and more compassionate people.

May the Lord bless all the job seekers and finders, this summer and always.

TIKKUN OLAM

"Then God said, 'Let there be Light'; and there was light."

--Genesis 1:3

How was your day? Today was a "bad parent" day for me. But then, I often have "bad parent", "sloppy worker" or "crummy wife" days. Yes, when it comes to taking guilt trips I must have a very good travel agent.

When I can't sleep at night, the TV in my head is well-stocked with episodes of *America's Biggest Mess-ups*, starring me. Adulthood has provided a rich mine of regret, remorse and embarrassment. When the adult memories have been played, I can reach back into my youth for a wealth of other examples. Take the time I forged my father's signature on a test paper. I was in first grade, and I think the "Tom Cunningham" in all printed capital letters probably tipped off Sister Vincent Maria. Then there was the eternal fighting with my parents and sisters, so very often instigated by me. I'd bend Father Farriker's ear with an impressive laundry list of sins in the confessional, then promptly go out and do it all again, sometimes starting before I even got out of church.

On other restless nights, as a change of pace from guilty, I just feel sad. Sad that the world is such a mess. Sad that my kids will inherit that mess. Sad that I am so very ill-equipped to do anything much about it.

But I have heard of something beautiful and inspirational, a thought to help banish some of my shadows. It the Jewish concept of Tikkun Olam. The English translation is "repairing the world." Here is the Jewish legend that inspired Tikkun Olam. It seems that, early in history, something happened to shatter the light of the universe. It broke into millions of pieces, and became millions of sparks living in all of creation. Mankind's great purpose is to look for, and collect, those pieces of light in each corner of the earth. The sparks that dwell in all the people we see, all the people whose lives we touch. In gathering up the light, we each play a part in repairing the world.

It is our purpose in life. Every one of us. We can each do our part. In fact, we are called to do our part. We are, it turns out, both capable and qualified. It begins by finding and honoring our own sparks of light from the universe. For me, mine might be found by peeking under the layers of excessive self-criticism, which after all is a form of self-pity. And, having found our sparks, we can live into our grand purpose, our divine calling. We can spend our days here searching for light, for goodness: in our families, our friends, our neighbors, and, yes, our enemies.

So, some nights now, when I can't sleep, I think of another image. I see myself, I see all of us, gently gathering up the light around us, fireflies twinkling in the darkness. I see the ball of light growing bigger and bigger with each small, but vital, contribution to the effort. I feel my own inner light growing stronger, illuminating even the darkest corners of my soul. When I think of Tikkun Olam, I feel a new power, the power of a very imperfect child to nevertheless help restore this imperfect world to divine perfection, the shining whole it was meant to be. There is very little room for sadness and self-pity in a life charged with such an important task.

Let's get busy. All of us, the guilty and sad, the wounding and wounded. There's so much light out there to be found. And we have our job to do. It's time to repair the world.

THE VIEW FROM THE MOOD SWINGS

"My days are swifter than a runner; they flee away, they see no good."

--Job 9:25

Picture this:

You wake up with your heart pounding, after only a few hours of sleep. You are energized, filled with exciting ideas and plans. You turn on the light to write page after page after page. You suggest amazing trips to incredible destinations. You feel, literally, you could do anything, with anyone.

You are wildly in love with the world. You feel beyond wonderful.

Picture this:

A week later, or a day later, or later that same day...

You start your downhill slide. You are so tired you can hardly function. You have no ideas, no plans, no interest in writing. No interest in anything. You feel, literally, that you couldn't do anything if your life depended on it. Paris, Rome, Bangkok—nowhere tempts you to travel. You feel drab and dismal. You feel far, far beyond sad. You feel hopeless.

Picture repeating this cycle, over and over, with the mood swings getting closer and closer together.

When you picture this, you are picturing bipolar disorder , also known as manic depression.

When you picture this, you are picturing me.

By the time I finally hit bottom and went to a psychotherapist, I had probably been suffering for about 30 years. Sometimes it takes me a little while to get broken things fixed. For 30 years I pushed aside my intuition that there was something wrong. After all, for the longest time these mood swings didn't happen that often. I could handle this, yes?

The dirty little secret of bipolar disorder is the seductive nature of the manic phase. For so many years I had counted on those jags of excitement and energy to get so, so many things done. I was the one who came up with the best birthday parties, the actress who memorized the shows in only hours, the great room mother, the ultimate multi-tasker. I got a lot of positive feedback for this, and I came to love feeling "up," and to endure the many, many lows that were the inevitable down side.

It was finally time for the whole house of cards to come crashing down. My crash happened in April. Rose was in Thailand; my mom had some very scary health issues, including recovering from a broken hip. There were money worries. The pressure built and built. The moods cycled closer and closer together. One morning I woke up—and the happy wild bipolar girl was utterly gone. I was all sadness, all tears for days and days at a time. The mania had lost its beauty and fun. It, too, was grotesque and out of control.

Within 24 hours I was (finally!) seeking professional help. Now I was traveling down a long and frightening road—a road of talking and talking, of taking lithium and other meds several times a day. What the heck was happening to me, me who didn't even take Tylenol after childbirth, for God's sake?

What was happening was not a choice. What was happening would never be anyone's choice.

Bipolar disorder has been identified as a chemical imbalance in the brain. While talking through problems with a therapist is hugely helpful, the chemical imbalance is the reason drug therapy is also necessary. I am taking "mood stabilizers" for moods that have not been stable for a very long time.

Well, here it is August. It has been a time marked by terror and hope, by a very successful mission trip to Alaska and the many failures of everyday life. It has been a time when I've been rendered breathless by the love of my family, who stuck with me even when I was very, very nasty (another charming side effect of this cursed disease).

Here it is, August. I am so much closer to getting well. Every day I feel more motivated, more capable of overcoming this. I look at September ahead, and I see that I am still on the roller coaster. I have always hated roller coasters. But I don't hate my life. Down as I get, I still deeply believe God has a plan for me here.

Being bipolar, I have tasted the wild extremes of life. It has been both agonizing and ecstatic. Life has its difficult and sad moments for us all. We all have our own private agonies and ecstasies. When we meet each other, in church or on the street, we may or may not know each other's pain. But the kind word, the smile, the squeeze of a hand-- these loving gestures are a lifeline for someone, more often than we may ever know.

Manic depression has just about worn me out. But in my heart I know there is still much more to give, so I'll keep fighting this.

Picture me: better.

IT'S ALL GOOD

"Honest balances and scales are the Lord's; all the weights in the bag are his work."

--Proverbs 16:11

For years, I didn't watch TV. At all. I don't count watching my little ones watch *The Big Comfy Couch* and *Arthur*. That was just babysitting, making sure PJ did not swallow the batteries in the remote, that Julie did not jam videotapes backwards into the VCR and hit "play" (by the way, *Pocahontas* did meet that fate). Once in a blue moon I would view *Masterpiece Theatre*, or a TV biography of some obscure physicist. No, my evenings were for classical music and Proust. When I heard colleagues or fellow train-riders talk about the latest episode of *Survivor*, I wallowed in my high-falutin' ignorance. TV was the opiate of the masses, after all. The time-sucker par excellence. The hypnotic force that drew families, trance-like, toward its fatuous, flickering images.

Well, this past year has been my come-uppance in a million different ways. To quote the Arctic Monkeys (you see?) "Whatever People Say I Am, That's What I'm Not." Me, the snooty anti-shopper, owner of three pairs of shoes, all down-at-heels, has suddenly become a capital "S' Shopper, owner of...well, let's just say "several" pairs of shoes. The makeup minimalist (did Chapstick count?) has become Ulta and Sephora's very best customer.

And Ms. Anti-TV watches it. A lot.

I pretty much watch it all, but my favorites are what I call the "nice" reality shows. Mr. Trump can go take a hike; the monstrous brats of *My Super Sweet Sixteen* can party on without me. But I am a pushover for shows like *Extreme Makeover, 10 Years Younger, Project Runway*. I love to see struggling families gasp in awe and delight as their homes are renovated, their hope restored. I cheer for the sweet, slightly shlumpy woman whose day of magic erases the years care etched on her face, and now looks 30 instead of 40 (where do I apply for that one?) And what <u>hasn't</u> been said about *Project Runway*? If you had any idea how many young people have returned to the sewing machine because of that show…it is truly inspirational! Well, maybe not to me. My only set of sewing lessons ended with my final project, plaid bell bottoms, sewn together both backwards and inside out.

My point? Well, I have been swimming in the high cultural deep end for a very long time. Believe me, Stephen Hawking and Camus are pretty heavy going for someone like me. I was dogpaddling in the intellectual 9 foot section of the pool. While I truly loved, and love, the stimulation of Scriabin and Matisse, Mahler and Faulkner, sometimes I needed…well, less. And I refused to see that.

I completely believe that God has a lesson for me in all this, written in giant letters. The pleasures of this world come in all sizes, and on all levels. To draw a line in the sand, and excoriate "low" culture, is to miss out on, as I've learned, a very great deal. Today's new young bands have raw energy, powerful music and terrific lyrics. Today's young people express themselves on YouTube, in blogs, on MySpace pages. Their performance art is often riveting. And yes, some of the new TV programs out there are moving, hilarious and completely original—or just plain fun to watch.

The same would be true on the other side of the line. So many people think they aren't "smart" enough to listen to certain music, to read certain books. They allow themselves to become so intimidated by "high" culture that they miss the gorgeous world of Brahms and Dali altogether. These riches are available to anyone who cares to reach, just a little. If people think they aren't entitled to reach, that is a tragedy.

Like Alice, I have fallen down a rabbit hole and come to understand the wonders of a different world. I've also come face to face with a different version of myself. And you know what? All it has done is to make me more excited about a world so rich and diverse, so "high." So "low." So beautiful. All it has done is to make me fall more in love with the God who made all of this, who made all of us.

My Evan often says something I try to keep in mind: "It's all good."

When we embrace culture (high, low and in between), when we respect one another's taste and opinions, and even dare to change our minds sometimes, it is, indeed, all good.

Beauty and the Geek is on in 10 minutes. Would you please pass the popcorn?

JOANIE TIME

"Every man's memory is his private literature."

--Aldous Huxley

Last week marked six months since Mom died. Half a year since she last came out to the kitchen to make a cup of tea. 32 weeks since watching the last episode of her beloved *Dr. Phil*. 180 days since Mom last told Julie she loved her.

And now it seems time is picking up speed, that we are moving faster and farther away from the reality of Mom living with us. I no longer absentmindedly set her place at the table every night (just some nights). Most of her things—clothes, books—are gone or stored now. Nana's room, while still called that, has become the guest bedroom. It's amazing how quickly the physical signs of 80 years of living can disappear. We are, all of us, so easily erased from this earth.

Which is why it is so, so important to make and share memories with those we love. My mom hated to cook, was a dreadful housekeeper and could never drive a car. But she was a queen of conversation, of memory making and keeping. If one of us girls needed a shoulder to cry on, or just someone to share a bit of good news, Joanie would be 100% there, in the moment with us. No matter that dinner, usually a dinner of the TV variety, burbled and eventually burned. No matter that the sharing took place on a sofa that also held newspapers, a full ashtray, and a plate from someone's afterschool snack. Maybe a Barbie doll as well. Frankly, Joanie didn't much care. She had other priorities. Her priorities were us.

And the wheels that could have given her so much more independence? She long ago decided that she didn't need to travel far, because her words could take her, and us, to incredible places. We were often transported to the exciting New York of the 1940s, when Mom worked at NBC in Rockefeller Center. Or we'd be in the first grade classroom at Ursuline School when little Marie decided to only answer to her middle name (Joan), much to the nuns' frustration. Sometimes we'd be with her on her (many!) dates, dancing in glamorous dresses to big bands at the country club.

Joanie's memories of us as little girls were many and vivid, and we loved hearing them. But we most enjoyed the stories she passed on from her own mother. How my Grandma and Grandpa met: she laughed at how badly he sang at a church musicale; he called her the rudest girl he'd ever seen. True love ensued, of course. All about Ireland, where Grandma had lived for awhile. And about little Sheridan, Grandma's youngest brother, after whom my Sheridan is named, who died at age four.

Our baby books were filled with recipes and phone numbers, and photos were haphazardly "stored" in dresser drawers, mixed with blouses and scarves. But it really didn't matter as long as Joanie talked, and we listened. Listened to our family story, told over and over, until her memories became our memories too.

The house is quieter now, six months down the road. There is a little pain when Evan sits down at the piano to play Gershwin and Mom isn't perched beside him, applauding madly as if she were in a concert hall. It's been awhile since all of the kids were treated to Nan's unique brand of extravagant praise. The two graduations coming up, Sher's from college and Rosie's from high school, will be tinged with melancholy.

My house is much cleaner than the house of my childhood (and I'm no neatnik, believe me). But it will be their loss if our kids recall housekeeping and cooking, and forget the messy and complicated beauty of our family story. Mom, remind me. Remind me to keep the conversation going, from you through me to them. Making memories, after all, beats making beds. And taking time, lots of time, to share those memories was your greatest gift to us. Erased from this earth? Joanie? Not while we're around.

THE SPORTING LIFE

"Every generous act of giving, with every perfect gift, is from above, coming down from the Father of lights, with whom there is no variation or shadow due to change."

--James 1:17

Permit me a little brag. We have two, count them, two serious athletes in our house these days. This is news, coming as it does at the end of a rather long drought in that department. Oh, our older three eventually found sports they enjoyed and were good at. But this prowess came later in childhood for them. Traditionally, ours were the kids who played instruments. In a showdown of games vs. music, there was no contest.

Family memories include the opinion of little Rose: "I like playing left field. It's a good place to be when you're not into a lot of action." We also recall Sher's first T-ball hit, after which he ran straight to third base because there was too much commotion over at first. My Saturday morning sideline comments ran less to "All the way, honey! Great goal!" and more to "Stand up, sweetie! Put your shoe back on!"

Well, imagine my surprise when our "second shift" proved to be so darned sporty. PJ and Julie both, it seems, were born playing ball—all kinds of ball. From the get-go they possessed poise, confidence and acumen. They even knew where on the field they were supposed to be. When fellow parents asked us, "Is that one yours?" we could note with pride that "ours" was the one crossing the finish line, not the one picking the dandelions.

How could this be? One possible, partial, explanation is the sheer number of practices and games to which they were dragged in their early, formative years. It certainly can't be explained by parental energy—that left the building quite some time ago. Genes? Well, Steve was co-captain of his high school basketball team at the seminary, the "Three L Llamas." Keep in mind, though, there were only nine guys in his whole class. My P.E. career was a sad parade of blown leads, strikeouts, stumbles and falls. When I learned that she who was chosen last for the team, would someday, somehow, be first in the Heavenly Kingdom, I found it a great comfort. Indeed, one would have to reach all the way back to my Grandpa Berrigan to find a truly amazing athlete. Grandpa played for the Bronx Giants, and we actually have a photo of him standing next to Babe Ruth. So, let's just say it's been awhile between sports stars.

Whatever the reason, PJ and Jules are finding their path, and it's a markedly different path than the one the first three trod. We have swapped seats in the concert hall for seats on the bleachers, and are enjoying the change. We marvel at the variety of interests and gifts that exists in our family, five children of the same parents. We could never have predicted, or controlled, who would love what. They are as unique as their fingerprints, and we thank God for that. As parents, it becomes clearer every day that we are caretakers, not creators, of our children's personalities.

And so it is in each family, in each of us. Each a one-of-a-kind mix of qualities, quirks, aspirations and achievements. Each with something special to offer the Body of Christ….a sense of humor, a warm heart, a flair for painting, a deft touch on the piano. One is a whiz at building and fixing things. One is a top scorer on the court, a powerhouse in the goal. Each a delight to the heart of our Parent.

So look for us on Saturday mornings out on that soccer field. You'll know us because we are 20 years older than the other spectators who are cheering their firstborns. But, ancient as we are, we'll be cheering too, as Julie proceeds down the field (in the right direction!) and as PJ's kick puts the team ahead.

Hey, this sporting life is pretty cool.

TIMELESS

"We feel and know that we are eternal."

--Spinoza

Time after time. Time's up. Just in time. Time stands still. Time flies.

Does anybody really know what time it is?

My 35th high school reunion took place, without me, a few weeks ago in Atlanta. Luckily, I was able to get a glimpse of all the festivities on Facebook (yay technology), and I was…appalled. At myself. Aside from the dear friend who posted the pictures, I did not recognize a single soul. No one. Zip. Nada. I couldn't even read their nametags, so those were no help. Who is that jolly, bald and portly fellow? That graying grandmotherly type (yeah, yeah, I know, I could be a grandmother too) waving to the camera? Not a solitary clue!

Now, surely THEY would have all recognized ME. Right? Right?

But these were my friends! On graduation day in 1974 we hugged, we cried, we all swore we would never forget each other. We'd know each other anywhere…Mary Kay, Muff, May-May…and that was only a small fraction of the M's.

The thing is, inside, I still feel like 17. In my heart. In my mind. A LOT.

The camera, however, doesn't lie.

Time has passed. A boatload of it.

Physically, we have all undergone massive changes. We inhabit bodies that have worked hard, maybe partied hard, gotten too much sun and not enough exercise. Bodies that have given birth. Bodies with parts that are starting to rebel—knees, hips, eyes, ears.

But there is a day, a year, a decade…a time in the past when we each still feel most at home, no matter how much time has passed since. For me that was (is) the early seventies. After rocking Woodstock, before catching Saturday Night Fever. As the Wheel of Fashion spins back to miniskirts and maxidresses—even gladiator sandals, of which I owned a particularly impressive pair—I nod appreciatively. A whiff of sandalwood incense, the first notes of "Color My World" by Chicago, and I am back where I belong.

Ironically, when I truly <u>was</u> 17, I used to be very impatient with the reminiscences of older people. Seriously, Grandma, the Depression is OVER (I would think to myself). Let's move on here! Yo, Uncle Gerry? The fifties? Ozzie and Harriet and hula hoops! Ancient history!

And now here I am, ever ready to discuss *Mary Tyler Moore* episodes, my 8-track tape collection and my extremely groovy poster of Pink Floyd's "Dark Side of the Moon."

It can be such a trap, you know. Worrying about time. And when thinking of Heaven and seeing departed loved ones again, it's easy to fall right into the trap. How old will they be? Will I even recognize them? How old will I look to them? Will they recognize me? Or will we be like the polite and puzzled strangers who reconnect at a Southern high school reunion, squinting at nametags and trying to remember?

This Thanksgiving month, I need to be grateful for the passage of time that brings me closer to the Divine Reunion. Some of us arrive at the reunion after 17 years, or 52, or 92. But we're all invited.

After that, I need to be grateful for, and freed by, the confidence that God transcends time. That eternal life with God is an utterly transcendent life. A life where everyone is a newborn, a teenager, a young parent, a wise elder…all at once. Where we live, at last, the life of the timeless soul.

It's OK to gaze in that mirror, or at those Facebook photos, with a pang of nostalgia for the way we were (and yes, "The Way We Were" was a big hit) in 1974. It's OK to wrestle with the concept of time, as long as we know it's not the only reality. We are destined to soar outside of time, beyond it. We were made to see the souls instead of the bodies.

So I might not know May-May from Adam if we meet again someday over white wine and spinach dip. But I believe, that, along with everything else we will know and understand there, we <u>will</u> all know each other in Heaven.

A Heaven of beautiful, of endless, of timeless, now.

MAYBE NEW YEAR

"That it will never come again / Is what makes life so
sweet."

--Emily Dickinson

The other night I looked on the computer at some of Rosie's cool
photos from the Thai New Year. While much of the world celebrates
the New Year when we do, several countries begin their year later in
winter, or even spring—April, in Thailand. And of course, they
celebrate differently. It is hard to beat the all-American tradition of
insane partying and fireworks (now THAT'S a sensible combination).
The great age divide is clearly marked between those who are IN Times
Square, or would be if they could, and those who look at Times Square
on TV and just do a lot of "tsk-tsking."

But maybe…maybe the unbridled joy of Songkran in Chiang Rai
would give us a run for our money. Thais kick off the New Year with a
three-day, nationwide, water fight. As Rose described it, all other
activity ceases as people splash each other with buckets of water, hoses,
water guns. It is pointless to even attempt to dry off, as the next water
blessing is just seconds away. Doesn't that sound awesome? The fact
that the temperature over there is 90 degrees probably enhances the
experience.

And what year IS it after all? Again, other cultures, other faiths, calculate differently. 2007 will be 5757 to our Jewish friends, 4705 to our Chinese neighbors.

Beyond the technical date, what is YOUR New Year? As a student, a mom, and in my current role here at church, September has always felt more like New Year's than January 1st. Our lives have cycles, unique cycles, that very often don't correspond to the calendar. So many of the "standard" dates carry a thousand pound burden of expectation. Christmas must be twinkling lights, an ocean of gifts, a time to be capital J Joyful. And we're slightly miffed when there isn't at least a dusting of snow. Easter is tricky—often we get that dusting of snow, but now we DON'T want it. We want spring blossoms, darn it!! Oh and those pesky relatives—they'd better get along this time!

When we try to force ourselves to feel certain ways just because, say, it's Halloween, we're doomed to disappointment. I personally gave up pretending to enjoy Halloween many full moons ago. For one thing, our family business of theatre has always ensured that every day is costume day. What tied it for me was the freezing, windy night when PJ was three. He saw the bowl filled with all of his VERY favorite candy, set on a table in his own toasty house. It fell to Mom to explain that no, he couldn't touch ANY of that. Instead, he'd have the fun of going out into the bitter cold night to get candy he might NOT like, from other people. "But," PJ asked with profound simplicity, "Why?"

As we (maybe) launch into our New Year's celebrations, it might be nice to relax if all does not go as planned. Let's try to remember that our carved-in-stone special holidays mean nothing to a huge part of the world. We each have an internal calendar to mark our days here. Birthdays, anniversaries, all unique to us. And equally important are the Everydays. If your heart lifts at the memory of a Tuesday night family dinner, all around the table, laughing, happy, blessedly safe another day….well then, isn't <u>that</u> your Thanksgiving? Far more, maybe, than the annual November high-stress clean-and-cook-athon?

Choose your special days. And don't be tyrannized by calendar dates. The dates are set, after all, by Man. But the days. Ah. The days are gifts from God.

Though I am considering a trip to Times Square on the 31st.

With buckets of water.

Wouldn't that be FUN?

CARVING OUT

"It is easy. You just chip away the stone that doesn't look like David."

> --Michelangelo (explaining how he made his statue of David)

Last week, during our mission trip to Vermont, we visited a marble quarry and carving studio. It was a New England summer evening (meaning the bugs were out en masse to enjoy it as well). In addition to a tour of the quarry, we were each given an opportunity to use carving tools and try to make our mark on stone. While some of the kids did an impressive job, the rest of us had to be satisfied with hacking off a miniscule chunk or two. A look around the outdoor sculpture garden, and at the beautiful works of art inside the studio, and we saw with new eyes the effort it takes to create a statue. As team leader Karin DeRuosi observed, sculpting is so different, because it is making art by taking away, not by adding.

It was a week of adding for us—we added buckets of dirt along a mountain trail, buckets of paint on a bridge, racks of clothes at the Salvation Army store, games and laughter in the Kids Club. We like to think we added something to the quality of life in Rutland by our work.

But when I look back, with new eyes, I see more beauty in what was taken away.

We arrived, tired but expectant, ready to be filled up with all the week had to offer. Hungry for fellowship, for fun, for hard work, for a deep spiritual experience. And every hour, there was a stripping away, an exposure of our weaknesses, our vulnerability. Every hour brought surprising developments, and as we had to adapt, we had to dig deep within ourselves for the resources.

We arrived without our technology: no cell phones, iPods, video games. No computers. No TV. And, despite some initial discomfort, we felt lightened. Lessened, in a good way. Less distracted. Less disengaged. Less encumbered by "stuff."

We arrived as the Christ's Lutheran Church group, and found we needed to blend with kids and adults from two other churches. The circumstances threw us into an immediate intimacy when we formed work crews together. As acquaintances blossomed into friendships, we dared to expose our true selves, at work, at play, at worship. There was a shedding of formality and pretense as we all plunged into this exciting new experience.

All of us had to shed our normal standards of cleanliness and grooming, as the extent of our daily beautifying ritual was an ice-cold three minute shower. I saw (and smelled) clothes that had been worked in. Hard. I saw hair untouched by blow-dryers, faces without makeup. Last week, these ornamentations were suddenly not important. And so they fell away.

It is easy to think of God as the Divine Painter, creating a breathtaking world of color and light and shape with His brilliant brush. Painting a rainbow. Adorning the trees with beautiful birds. But last week I came to see God as the Sculptor. We come to Him, solid flesh and blood. And He chips away. Hardships. Tragedies. All change us, take away our comfort and complacency—reduce our pride. Opportunities. Challenges. He chips some more pretense away, revealing strength within us. Compassion. Honesty. As He carves, something begins to emerge from the blocks of marble that we are. Our very essence. And, because of the artistry of the Sculptor, that essence shines. It is new, stripped down, exposed, revealed. And if we are willing to let God shape us, we can see even the harshest moments of life with new eyes. We were created, and are in the process of being re-created. God wants to make us beautiful works of art. And down at our very core, that is what we can become.

So maybe we are less than we were before we came to Rutland. But maybe, just maybe, less is a whole lot more.

NOTES FROM THE COMFORT ZONE

"Even youths will faint and be weary, and the young will fall exhausted; but those who wait for the Lord shall renew their strength, they shall mount up with wings like eagles, they shall run and not be weary, they shall walk and not faint."

--Isaiah 40: 30-31

It's 93 degrees in the shade—and it's still June. Local, national and international news is so upsetting that even this news junkie needs a break. The kids are slogging through the last week of school. Everyone—even perpetually sunny PJ—is cranky and snappish. Our family needs a vacation from life-as-we-are-living-it.

At times like these, we all retreat to our versions of the comfort zone—a place attached to fond memories, simpler expectations, a slower pace. Predictability, reliability, stability are the watchwords of the comfort zone. We're feeling tired and fragile. We need to be surrounded by things we can count on.

This is not the time to try weird new recipes for dinner. This is the time to prepare everyone's favorites, provided those favorites don't require heating up the kitchen.

These days, as our relatively strict school year TV rules begin to relax into summer ones, my kids' shows of choice tend to be the sitcoms they loved years and years ago. In fact, a rerun of *Boy Meets World* can be heard in the background as I write this—Rose is in serious comfort zone mode.

For me, it's just about time to reread *A Tree Grows in Brooklyn*, a book I discovered the summer I was 10 years old, and a never-ending source of joy every time I read the opening lines once more: *Serene was a word you could put to Brooklyn, New York. Especially in the summer of 1912.*

In the comfort zone, the succulent, buttery fresh corn we eat is the corn that takes Steve back home again to Indiana, that takes me back to the Jersey Shore, that takes Sheridan back to Lewes, Delaware, circa 1990.

In the comfort zone, a silly, funny TV show puts the children back in touch with the people they were when they first laughed at the jokes, sprawled on the family room floor many years ago.

In the comfort zone, a beloved book, so well known as to be nearly memorized, strips away layers of worry and world-weariness to reconnect me with the little girl I was when I first encountered this story.

There is, of course, a danger in thinking of church as our comfort zone too often. Christ clearly calls us, his 21st century disciples, to leave comfort behind, to take risky journeys for His sake, to reach out to others without dwelling on our own needs and preferences. And yet…

We need to hear the Gospel, over and over and over again. Our spirits thirst for it, and for the prayers we've known since we learned to speak, the hymns we sang in Sunday School. We crave the order of the service, the familiar words of the liturgy. We need, once in awhile, when the world overwhelms, frightens and exhausts us, to seek out the greatest Comforter. We need to sit in the pews like little children once more, feeling totally safe and loved.

And after our time in the comfort zone, we head back out into our lives again, ready to face a future that is anything but stable and predictable.

Three meals a day of corn on the cob, 24/7 marathons of old TV programs, a library of just one novel, a worship service that never changes or challenges us? Definitely NOT a good idea.

A little time in the comfort zone every now and then? Well, that may be just what the doctor ordered.

SHEER PERFECTION

"This moment contains all moments."

--C.S. Lewis

You know, it takes real effort to bowl a 36 game. You have to be, not just a poor, but an abysmal athlete. We kept mixing up teams so that no one would be stuck with me for too long. Everywhere I landed, the cumulative score sank like a stone. Meanwhile, the kids and Steve laughed and joked around, nonchalantly knocking down pin after pin. The ones who hadn't bowled in years bowled the games of their lives. Julie's score ranked right up there with the big kids'. I watched in amazement as Sheridan actually took a cell phone call during his turn—he strolled up, still talking to his caller, and proceeded to get a strike. Everyone had advice for me: *relax* (my personal favorite, as I literally do not know how to do this, ever), *twist your wrist a different way—not THAT way, Mom, step out with your right foot, Mom, focus on sending the ball right down the middle.* I tried every stance imaginable, several sizes of bowling balls—and still ended up in the gutter just about every time. It was frustrating. It was humiliating.

And if I had to come up with the perfect day, I'd search no farther than that one.

All five children were home for Christmas. After days of unpacking, visiting friends and generally rushing around, we'd taken this day to enjoy a rare outing together as a family.

After my induction into the Bowler's Hall of Shame, we proceeded down to Chinatown. As he had done in the past, Sher ordered for the table. With his host of Chinese musician friends, he is the go-to guy in an Asian restaurant. Salt-baked squid (it's incredible, trust me). Watercress in garlic sauce. Honey-walnut shrimp. I was on a much firmer footing in Shiao Lan Kung than I'd been at Thunderbird Lanes. I cannot bowl. I can, however, eat. The laughter and joking continued, not ALL at my expense. We shared nine different dishes, and by the end not a chopstick-full was left.

We were not exactly The Waltons when they were all little. Stomping up to rooms and slamming doors were regular features of family dinners at one point. We would sit in the pew in church on Sunday and try to hide the fact that, just minutes before: the baby had been crying, one had made the baby cry, two had been fighting in the back seat of the car, and one had been sulking, because she just HATED what I made her wear. At our worst moments, I envisioned them all leaving home in a collective huff, permanently scarred by their upbringing, never to be heard from again.

Yet somehow, they made it through childhood, and made their way to these great relationships with each other. And a magical day like this.

Almost immediately, they would begin to disperse once more— Sheridan back to New York City, Evan to South Carolina, Rosie to Boston. But just for a few fleeting moments, we were all present and accounted for, safe and sound. Together and happy. Aware of just how lucky we were.

What does Heaven look like to you? To me, it's a day like that, one perfect day, the day that makes the tough days—and years—worth slogging through. God treats us to them, every once in awhile. Of course, life on earth is never an unbroken string of days like these. Only Heaven is. But on these perfect days, we get a glimpse of what will be, someday, forever. It's up to us to stop and notice. And be glad.

In this bleak midwinter, I wish you bowling alleys and Chinese restaurants, and perfect days with the people you love.

READY OR NOT

"Be dressed for action and have your lamps lit; be like those who are waiting for their master to return from the wedding banquet, so that they may open the door for him as soon as he comes and knocks... You also must be ready, for the Son of Man is coming at an unexpected hour."

--Luke 12: 35-36, 40

Item found in my carry-on for my flight to Charleston to see Evan:
Fun and diverting reading material for a three hour wait in Atlanta Airport—

Noam Chomsky's *Hegemony or Survival*, a gift from Sheridan. My sweet kid has a flattering, but inflated idea of his mom's IQ. Mom cannot even define "hegemony." It's going to be a looong layover.

Items not found:

Sunscreen

Sunglasses

Sensible shoes

Toothbrush

I curse myself for this the next day, when I walk, sunburned and squinting, in 90 degree heat, all over Charleston, in patent leather flip-flops, looking for a place to buy a toothbrush.

I knew this trip was coming up. Really, I did. So why was I so unprepared?

It seems like I'm always trying to prepare for events, only to arrive at those moments with only some of what I need.

My sister Maureen, it could be said, was never ready for anything. The nuns at Our Lady of Perpetual Help School cut her lots of slack on turning in homework and taking make-up tests. But no matter how long a reprieve she got, it wasn't long enough to study for the test or do the assignment. Later in life, she'd run out of milk before the recipe was finished, run out of gas before she got to work, run out of money before the rent was due.

Mo probably didn't know when she woke up on September 30, 1981, that it would be her last day, that a car crash would end her earthly life late that night. So you can imagine, true to form, she wasn't prepared.

Will my last moments on earth feel like this, too? Getting to the airport with inadequate luggage? Out of time, out of food, out of gas?

Perhaps.

And yet…

As the years have passed, I've come to truly believe that Mo <u>was</u> fully packed. That she actually had plenty of what she needed for her trip. That she'd learned exactly the lessons she needed to know before embarking.

Even without my sunglasses and sensible shoes, the visit with Evan was absolutely wonderful. I had my son, so I did have all I really needed.

Christ says, "Therefore keep watch, because you do not know on what day your Lord will come." But the Lord knows. And I believe He is not <u>trying</u> to catch us unprepared. He calls us when we've learned the lessons we were put here to learn, whenever that might be.

The servants in Jesus' parable aren't perfect. But they are watching. Their lamps are lit. They are keeping their eyes out for their Master.

And maybe that's all that any of us can do. God knows when it's our time. And He runs to find us. If we keep watching, there will come the moment when our gaze will meet the Master's. He will look at us with forgiveness and the greatest, greatest love. And, "ready" or not, we'll be home at last.

BE HERE NOW

"You must live in the present, launch yourself on every wave, find your eternity in each moment."

--Henry David Thoreau

Breathing in, I know that I am breathing in. In through my nose.

Breathing out, I know that I am breathing out. Out through my mouth.

Soft music plays as I notice my scattered thoughts drifting through my head. And here's one of them, suddenly...

PJ, age four: "First I inhale, then I unhale!"

It catches me, this memory, the voice of my cheerful little guy telling me this at bedtime, putting on his "shamamas" after finishing his "sedert," nestling with so many Beanie Babies that he almost disappears in a sea of plush.

As a child, PJ was the King of the Present Moment. Occasionally those moments were sad, of course. I remember the day he accidentally let go of his balloon, and said, tears rolling down his cheeks, "It's OK. It's up there keepin' Grandpa company in Heaven!" But, an overwhelming majority of the time, PJ approached the world with unbridled joy and wonder. He greeted every new day with "Awesome!"

He heralded each plan for an outing (even a trip to the Acme!) with "Yessss!!! I KNEW it could happen!"

Of course, this is how little ones are. They laugh, they cry, they are fully present with every emotion, every second of their lives. As we age, we tend to lose that, some of us utterly. We live in a state of permanent distraction, suspended somewhere between yesterday and tomorrow, as minutes and hours, and then years, slip by un-noticed.

But here's the funny thing. Where some of his siblings (taking after their mother, of course!) stress and fret, plan and regret, PJ retains the now-ness of a child. As the years have passed, PJ has really never lost that deep, deep connection to the moment.

PJ at 18 is still a happy camper. Or a sad camper. But, always, a "present" camper. If he's having a good day at lacrosse, the heavens rejoice. If he's having a Bad Science or Math Moment, the heavens weep. But—and here's the trick—it's all just for now, and PJ understands that. It comes, it passes. He doesn't seem to spend a lot of time dwelling, or letting thoughts of an unknown future cause him too much anxiety. This approach to "being" may have a practical drawback or two. I do recall the honking of a many a carpool horn as Peej sat at the breakfast table, serenely contemplating his bowl of Honey-Nut Cheerios. But by and large, what a way to experience the fullness of life!

He returns for the weekend from college. Once more, a happy camper. He thoroughly enjoys his homemade dinner, his comfy bed, the washer and dryer that will launder his mountain of clothes, watching Navy beat Notre Dame on TV with his dad. He hunkers down and revels in the present moment.

Buddhists would say this is the source of true happiness. Awareness. Mindfulness. Emptying the mind of projections, past and future. Reveling in the sight of the sun, the feel of that sun on your face, the taste and smell of a delicious bowl of soup, the sound of a loved one's voice.

I struggle mightily with this, this mindfulness. Most of the time I'm multitasking—simultaneously obsessing about yesterday's goof-ups and dreading the probable goof-ups of tomorrow. It's so hard for me to be here, now. Even as I know that "now" is all there really is.

But this morning, I sit in the meditation room at peace, at ease. For a change, I can concentrate on what I'm feeling. Right this second. And

I'm feeling a bubbling up of love and thanks for PJ, and the lesson he's teaching me with his everyday life. And in my mind's ear I hear my loved one's voice. The sweet voice of a four year old. The deep, all-grown-up voice of an 18 year old. Welcoming me to here.

Inhaling, I know that I am inhaling.

Unhaling, I smile.